SELF MOTIVATION
STRATEGIES
FOR WOMEN

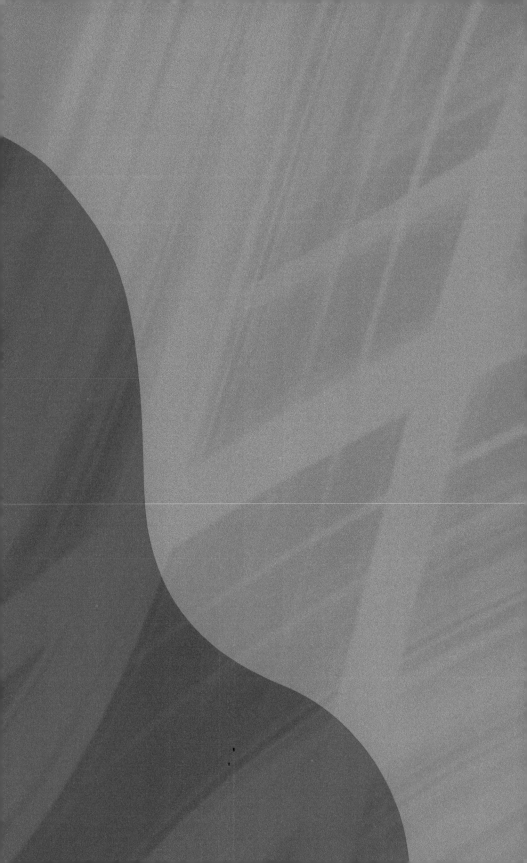

Self Motivation Strategies

FOR WOMEN

How to Achieve Your
Goals to Transform Every
Aspect of Your Life

Jen Rulon

ROCKRIDGE
PRESS

To my mom, who showed me how to live with heart.
To my niece, Taryn, who taught me to dance again.
To the women who are trying to harness their inner
strength and find their freedom to change.

For general information on our other products and services or to obtain technical support, please contact our Customer Care Department within the United States at (866) 744-2665, or outside the United States at (510) 253-0500.

Rockridge Press publishes its books in a variety of electronic and print formats. Some content that appears in print may not be available in electronic books, and vice versa.

TRADEMARKS: Rockridge Press and the Rockridge Press logo are trademarks or registered trademarks of Callisto Media Inc. and/or its affiliates, in the United States and other countries, and may not be used without written permission. All other trademarks are the property of their respective owners. Rockridge Press is not associated with any product or vendor mentioned in this book.

Interior and Cover Designer: Jennifer Hsu
Art Producer: Sue Bischofberger
Editor: Carolyn Abate
Production Editor: Ashley Polikoff

Author photo courtesy of Vanessa Velazquez Photography

ISBN: Print 978-1-64876-623-7
eBook 978-1-64876-122-5

R0

Contents

INTRODUCTION _____ vi

PART ONE: TAKING STOCK _____ 1

    CHAPTER ONE: All Right, Let's Do This _____ 3

    CHAPTER TWO: Setting the Stage _____ 21

PART TWO: DOING THE WORK _____ 37

    CHAPTER THREE: You Don't Have to Run a
    Marathon, but Get Active *(Health and Wellness)* _____ 39

    CHAPTER FOUR: Emotional Resilience Is More
    Than Feelings *(Emotional Health)* _____ 57

    CHAPTER FIVE: There's No Such Thing as a
    Tribe of One *(Personal Relationships)* _____ 77

    CHAPTER SIX: Get Your Frida Kahlo On *(Creativity)* _____ 95

    CHAPTER SEVEN: What Would Your Most
    Successful Friend Do? *(Career and Wealth)* _____ 111

    CHAPTER EIGHT: Are You There, Higher Power? *(Spirituality)* ___ 129

    CHAPTER NINE: Community Isn't Just a TV Show
    (Volunteering, Donating, Taking a Stand) _____ 143

    CHAPTER TEN: Staying the Course *(Making Good Habits Stick)* ___ 161

REFERENCES _____ 167

RESOURCES _____ 182

INDEX _____ 188

Introduction

It is the final afternoon of Hurricane Sally, September 2020. I am sitting in my condo in Destin, Florida, on the Gulf Coast. I came here to finish up this book, gain a clear head, sit with myself, and scout out places for a women's retreat. Ironically, prior to writing this book, I had to weather my own storm on a personal and professional level.

During November 2019, in Panama City Beach, Florida, I completed my fifteenth Ironman Triathlon, a brutal 2.4-mile swim, 112-mile bike, and 26.2-mile run, all combined into one never-ending race. Two years prior, I raced at the Ironman World Championship in Kona, Hawaii. In Panama City Beach, I accomplished my personal best. But I knew that would be my *last* race. My gut was telling me that that chapter of my life was over. I felt a major sense of accomplishment, but I was also scared.

You see, during those years between my first race in 1992 and my last in 2019, my life was swim, bike, run, repeat. Racing wasn't just my passion; it became my job. I got a master's in kinesiology, and I started my business as a performance triathlon coach. I used my Instagram and Facebook following to post racing, training, and nutrition tips and tricks. My social media presence propelled me into the spotlight as a much-coveted speaker for my coaching perspective, my journey as an athlete, and my business insight. But, as I crossed that finish line in November 2019, all the experience and expertise that grounded my business—and frankly, my identity—was about to dissolve.

What did I want to do moving forward? I knew I wanted to continue helping people, to make an impact, but could I do that in a way that was separate and different from my current identity? My priorities were changing. As I was running on the beach in Costa Rica a month after the race, bawling my eyes out because I felt lost and scared, a revelation came to me: I didn't need Ironman to fuel my soul—I'd had that drive in me my entire life. I gave myself the space to uncover my next meaningful chapter: helping women "find their champion status from within," whatever their goals may be. I started working with women who wanted to elevate their lives, who wanted to find the drive to become the best versions of themselves, and who wanted to figure out what fuels them—what motivates them to become champions in all aspects of their lives. This is how my Monarch Mindset Program began.

Even though my previous business was focused on endurance and training, I've uncovered many lessons that translate to any woman who is eager to live her best life—from tapping into your emotional health and spirituality to finding your creative expression and sense of self-worth to investing in your community, as well as in your health and wellness. In this book, I will help you examine all these areas of your life so that you can motivate yourself to make whatever changes are necessary to arrive at and achieve your best. In part one, you'll have an opportunity to determine where you are now and where you want to go. Then, in part two, for each area of life, I'll offer a variety of motivating techniques and practical tips, ranging from simple list-making, time chunking, to mindfulness and meditation strategies to keep you motivated and on track when the day seems to beat you down. I'll also share stories of my amazing clients and how they found their motivation, with the hope that you'll recognize a little bit of yourself. Overall, my goal is to help you sort out where you are truly thriving and where you are merely surviving and then find ways to motivate yourself to thrive in life as a whole.

As you move through this book, you may end up enduring your own hurricane. I don't mean literally, like I am doing right now—the rain has stopped, but the winds are crazy strong. To put it bluntly, there will beautiful moments and there will be really shitty moments. Please know that I am here to ride out that storm with you. I've tackled my own storms, and I'm excited to help you through yours. Finding the right motivation and strategies to become the best version of yourself—no matter how challenging—is truly worth the journey.

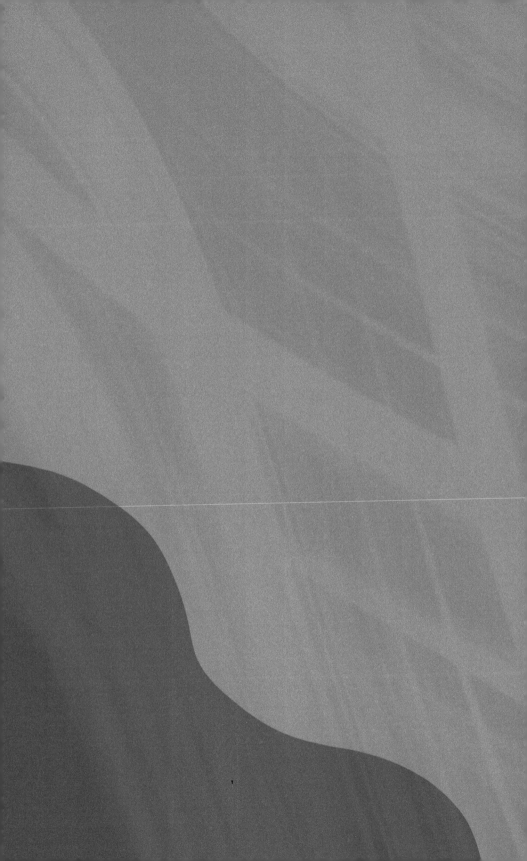

PART ONE

Taking Stock

CHAPTER ONE

All Right, Let's Do This

As you are about to start your journey, whatever that may be—a new job, losing 15 pounds, or starting your own business—let me be frank: It will take work, time, and grit. But that is why you picked up this book, right? This chapter focuses on the secrets to finding your motivation for change. I want you to look deeply at where you are, right now. We'll address how you got here and where you want to be, but with none of the typical self-help BS. Don't get me wrong, self-reflection is important, but I'm more of an action-oriented person who wants actual tips once I've envisioned what I want.

The Secret to Motivation

The secret sauce to creating change in your life isn't a mystery. It is all about staying motivated to sustain that change. Planning, dreaming, and reflecting on your life's transformation is one thing. Figuring out what strategies work to get you to your end goal and to stay there is essential. But it takes time to discover which motivational strategies are best for you. For example, your best friend may live and die by list-making and planning out her every move by the hour. You, on the other hand, may respond to timed work sprints to get through as much as you can, with a reward of a walk around the block. Making a change in any life circumstance is not only challenging but also scary. It's the unknown. It can and will happen, but it will take preparation and true commitment.

Knowing what methods work to help you stay on top of your goals is the most crucial part of your motivation equation. This is true when life is grand and beautiful and when life is challenging and discouraging. I mean, it's easy to stay motivated when life is filled with rainbows and butterflies, so to speak. But staying motivated after you've lost a job or a loved one, or when a plan simply isn't going according to your dream timeline? Now that takes true determination. In this book, I have tips and tools to draw on in both light and dark times to help you stay motivated. I have mixed simple tips with more evidence-based strategies for you to try out. I've culled together quite a collection because I want to ensure everyone has the opportunity to find what resonates with them. Before we begin, make sure you have a journal dedicated to this book; as there will be lots of exercises throughout, you will be doing a lot of reflecting, writing, and planning.

Are you ready to get started?

Exercise: What's Going On?

Take this book to your favorite spot. No distractions. No kids, no dogs, no job, no partner, no parents, no friends. Just you and the world. I'm here and happy to wait. You settled in? Good.

Take this opportunity to think about a particular situation in your life and any issues that rise up with it that you want to change. Pull out your journal and start writing down your thoughts, along with some action steps you can take. Remember, there are no wrong responses. Also, don't erase anything—you wrote it down for a reason. Keep it so you can look back later and assess the progress you've made. Here are some short examples to get you started (yours can be as long as you need them to be):

- I'm bored at work. My job is just not challenging enough, and I know I can do so much more. I need to work on my résumé, make connections on LinkedIn, and start scheduling interviews by *(fill in date)*.

- I feel like I've lost myself. I've been so busy taking care of others that I've neglected my own needs. I want to find *me* again. I've always had a dream to start my own business, and now is the time. I'll get the process rolling by *(fill in date)*.

- I've put on 25 pounds over the past few years, and I'm starting to feel sluggish and uncomfortable in my skin. It's affecting my energy level and even my desire to get out and socialize. I am sick of making excuses for why I can't lose weight. I'm going to start an exercise program and a healthy-eating plan by *(fill in date)*.

Once you finish writing, take a minute to review the area you want to change. How are you feeling with those thoughts? Good? Terrible? Frustrated? Feeling a bit unsettled by it all? That's okay. You are human. I'm going to go ahead and guess you are staring at the paper and wondering, "How am I going to make a change?" or "How will I stay motivated?" You may have already started telling yourself, "No way I will make this happen" or "This is going to take forever."

I know how hard it can be to look at the big picture, so pat yourself on the back for taking this initial step. Nearly 15 years ago, I was in your shoes. I had my childhood dream job of working with marine mammals. After more than a decade, I realized it wasn't fulfilling anymore. I wanted to go back to school to get my master's in kinesiology and start my own business. The idea of leaving my job was scary. I can't tell you how many times I heard, "Why would you leave your dream job?" Sigh. I knew in my heart that I had accomplished everything I wanted in that job. I also knew I wasn't going to let other people's fears overshadow my decision. My motivation? My career goals had changed. I wanted a job that would help others achieve their dreams.

Now go back to your journal and reflect on these questions:

1. Why do you want to make a change in your life? Identify your reason. For example, if you want a new job, is it to be able to use your skills and expand your knowledge to feel richer in experience? Is it because you want to use your talents to help others?

2. What is the limiting factor holding you back from achieving your goal? For example, if you're bored at work but haven't taken any steps to get a new job, is it because you might be lacking in self-confidence? Figuring out what's holding you back will take some time, so prepare to get really honest with yourself here.

You'll have more opportunities throughout the book to gain insight into the changes you want to make and how to go about motivating yourself to make them. For now, becoming aware of what you want to change and your initial goals for making that change is the first step on your journey.

A Self-Help Book for the 21st Century

I'm not going to promise you the golden ticket to success. More important, I don't want to. What I do want is to offer you practical, engaging tools and methods so you can turn your life around, no matter your situation.

One of the most important steps in this process is to figure out who you turn to for motivation. Do you reach out to girlfriends or jump on social media to search for inspiration? Perhaps you turn to a website such as Pinterest and put together an inspiration board for yourself. Many women like to connect with other women, because we know that women are *way* more alike than society leads us to believe.

But, as you know, it wasn't always this way. Society doesn't always allow women the freedom to make their own life decisions, so there hasn't always been a need for casual groups of female CEOs who come together once a month to share best practices; or more formal organizations such as Girls Who Code, which encourages young girls to pursue careers in computer science; or WeCOACH, which has pushed for more female coaches in male-dominated sports.

My examples here are very specific, but that's the point. Women have a lot more choices now than our grandmothers ever did. And, as this world continues to evolve, we see more women inspiring and supporting other women—helping them take a stand, sharing their voices, and cheering them on when they succeed. The idea of being "threatened" by another woman isn't so much of a thing anymore (sans *The Real Housewives*), as most women are helping others place their crowns high atop their heads. Social media in particular has played a huge role in amplifying our successes. I see women every day, inspiring me, in real life and online. Be it a woman who inspires us because:

- She stepped up and spoke the truth about her experience on live television even though many people refused to believe her story.

- She works tirelessly to inspire people to explore their own self-worth and value.

- Even though she's an international movie star, she always wanted to complete a triathlon, and did.

These are all real-life women. Can you guess who I am talking about? Send me an email if you've figured it out!

The Enjoli Woman

In the 1970s, following the women's movement, an unforgettable commercial entered our collective lives. The main character was a beautiful woman who sang, "I can bring home the bacon. Fry it up in a pan. And never, never, never let you forget you're a man." Apparently, she worked, took care of the family, and had a fantastic sex life, all with grace and ease. She wore Enjoli perfume, which was supposed to embody all that the women's movement promised.

Sure, it's 2021 now, and the Enjoli-woman archetype is long gone, but let's be real, the media still has a ways to go. Luckily, there are real women making real changes in our world.

- Malala Yousafzai, an advocate of women's rights, won the Nobel Peace Prize at age 17.
- Judith Butler, a philosopher and gender scholar, has written books on feminist and LGBTQIA+ topics.
- Kamala Harris is the first African American, first Asian American, and first female vice president.
- Serena Williams, who has won 23 Grand Slam titles, is not only a tennis star but has battled against gender and racial bias.
- Stay-at-home moms everywhere, who are able to take care of their kids, their houses, and their partners, with little time for their own self-care, however they define it, and still make themselves a prioriy.

While we have come a long way since commercials like Enjoli, we still have strides to make. Think back to 2017, when the Me Too movement exploded. Women of all ages, races, sexual orientations, and nationalities came together to *finally* talk about how they, too, had been sexually assaulted. Equal pay is also still an issue for women. Today, white women earn 82 cents for every dollar of what white men make. Women of color earn just 75 cents. According to the American Association of University Women, the pay gap will not close until 2093. (There's more about career and worth in chapter 7.)

The 1970s Enjoli commercial showed how "perfect" women were when, in reality, many of us were dealing with struggles that weren't talked about. I'm happy to see that we are working to avoid that same trap today. Sure, the world isn't always supportive and helpful, but as women, it's our duty to help one another. I'm happy to be doing my part in supporting you.

Exercise: Your Priority Pie

Have you ever looked at your life and thought, "Man, I have it together! Everything I embody—family life, career, physical health, social life, cultural outings and events, and emotional well-being—is balanced, equal, and just." Yeah, me neither. But it doesn't mean we can't try!

If you're looking to improve your life, it's important to take the time to figure out where you spend your time between work, family, health, and other activities. Some of these choices are not always within your control. They're often fueled by circumstances and responsibilities. In other cases, you can take control by setting priorities and creating opportunities. To get a better sense of where you'd like your priorities to be, it's essential to know where your current priorities land.

Grab your journal. On a fresh page, draw a large circle representing a pie. Consider the following "slices":

- Community
- Creativity
- Family
- Mental Health and Wellness
- Physical Health
- Spirituality
- Work

Slice your pie into pieces that represent the portions of your life (day or week) that you spend on each category. It's highly unlikely your slices will be equal. Think about how much time you spend working (in the office *and* at home), chauffeuring kids or running errands, working out, reading for pleasure, etc. Categories that take up a lot of your time should be bigger slices and vice versa.

Once you've completed your pie, take some time to process what's in front of you. What does your Priority Pie look like? What pieces of your life do you focus on most? Is this how you want your pie to look? If not, draw another circle. Ask yourself, "How do I want my pie to look?" Now, divide the pie up the way you want your life to be. This will help you gain the motivation needed to make changes for yourself as you work through the book.

A Healthy Dose of Reality

Now that you have a better understanding of where you want to be in your life, it's time to think about what you can accomplish and how. For example, maybe you want to exercise but can't afford a gym membership, so you haven't started a workout regimen. Or what if you want more time for self-care but you need to take care of aging parents or young children? If something is in your way, you may think you don't have a choice. But you *do* have options. We all have the same hours in our days, and we see a ton of people succeed by making choices and figuring shit out. These people make their goals a priority, and you can, too.

"Ninety-nine percent of the failures come from people who have a habit of making excuses."

—GEORGE WASHINGTON CARVER

A common example that I hear is from clients who want to get in shape and lose weight but complain they can't afford a gym membership. The reality is, there are thousands of fitness trainers online providing *free* Zoom workouts. From Instagram Live, IGTV, and YouTube to Facebook and the app lululemon athletica, the options are endless. When it comes to fitness, another common excuse is not having the time. However, if you want to see changes, fitness must be nonnegotiable. You might need to get your booty out of bed an hour earlier to prioritize fitness.

A couple of years ago, I worked with Lyndze, a client who'd been sitting on her business idea for almost two and a half years, because she didn't set realistic goals and make them a priority. Her excuse was that there was way too much on her plate to make anything happen. Together, we broke down the key components she needed to kick-start her side hustle:

1. Come up with a business name and register it.

2. Set up the legal aspects of the business.

3. Get the URL name and build a website.

4. Find a logo designer.

5. Build a prototype.

Within three months, she had set the foundation of her business and was well on her path toward success.

How to Talk Yourself into Anything

Do you have a list of inspiring quotes that motivate you when you need to face a challenge? Some days I feel frustrated or tired and honestly not motivated, so I pull out one of my favorite quotes (I used it in my TEDx Talk) and say it to myself: "Champions keep playing until they get it done right." The author of this quote is Billie Jean King; she won 39 Grand Slam titles and is an advocate for gender equality. Her words inspire and motivate me to keep going. In essence, they talk me into facing the moment or the day with renewed incentive.

I want you to have some quotes you can turn to when you need to change your mindset, too, and talk yourself into getting your butt in gear. You can use Billie Jean King's quote or any of the following. Write them down in your journal and look for others that resonate with you. Say them to yourself when you know you need to do something but just don't feel motivated. Use them frequently as you work through this book to talk yourself into moving forward.

"What you're supposed to do when you don't like a thing is change it. If you can't change it, change the way you think about it. Don't complain."

—MAYA ANGELOU, AMERICAN POET AND CIVIL RIGHTS ACTIVIST

"The greatest danger to our future is apathy."

—JANE GOODALL, PRIMATOLOGIST, ENVIRONMENTAL ADVOCATE, AND ANIMAL ACTIVIST

"I have chosen to no longer be apologetic for my femininity. And I want to be respected in all of my femaleness. Because I deserve to be."

—CHIMAMANDA NGOZI ADICHIE, AUTHOR OF *WE SHOULD ALL BE FEMINISTS*

"No one can make you feel inferior without your consent."

—ELEANOR ROOSEVELT, FORMER FIRST LADY OF THE UNITED STATES AND HUMAN RIGHTS ACTIVIST

You Can Walk and Chew Gum at the Same Time

Sometimes the most challenging part of making life changes is navigating the spaces of the life you already have. Here's a common scenario: You want to get a new job, but you have to continue to work in your current position to make the money you need for everyday expenses. You are living life as you know it while adding more responsibilities to your plate—you have to put together your résumé, make connections on social media and business platforms, and write follow-up emails.

The idea of taking on more responsibility is one of the most common reasons people stop short of achieving change. Why add more to your plate when you don't know if this is what you should do or even if you will find a better job? Because it will likely be worth it! I know from experience that figuring out how to move forward is a delicate balance. Here are some motivation tips to help get you past the obstacles in the way of making change happen:

Add more productivity time to your schedule. Think about how you spend your time. For example, is it essential for you to binge-watch the newest Netflix series, or spend hours a day on social media platforms? Can you steal back time from something in your life that's not getting you where you want to go so that you can devote additional time to making the changes you want? Figure out where you can cut back on nonessentials to be more productive.

Use the resources you have. When you have an interest that you want to pursue, one of the best ways to get started is to look in your own backyard. For example, one of my clients works for a large corporation. She's a big believer in volunteering, so she scours the company's community initiatives to find programs that are a good fit for her interests. While she maintained her full-time job, she also started volunteering with nonprofits and used her consulting skills by assisting women with building their résumés and finding jobs.

Connect with your online community. When you seek to grow and change, who better to help you than people who are on a similar path? For example, normally a social butterfly, my client Elizabeth struggled through the 2020 COVID-19 lockdown. When she started working from home and couldn't go out socially anymore, she missed being around people. What did she do? She found online groups of like-minded individuals, connected with my program, and jumped on a dating site. She's made some fantastic friends and even met a man she likes!

Exercise: Flip Through Your Successes

In this exercise, you're going to flip through the Rolodex of your successes. Too young to know what a Rolodex is? Think of all the contacts on your phone organized on small index cards fastened to a rotating device that you can spin around to find the contact you want. (Times were much simpler before smartphones!)

Pull out your journal and find a quiet spot. Play some soothing music, think of these topics, and journal about them:

- A time when you were a child and you accomplished something you were proud of (e.g., learned how to ride a bike, got an A+ on a paper, bought something you wanted with your own money). How did you feel that day? How did you feel that week?

- A time when you were scared to do something because you didn't know if the outcome was going to be a "win," but it turned out well (e.g., afraid to love again after getting hurt but ended up in a successful relationship).

- A time when you used your skills to help yourself move forward (e.g., offered knowledge outside your department and got offered a different position with higher pay for the skills you displayed).

- A time you said to yourself, "Enough is enough. I need to make a change NOW," and you did (e.g., dropping 20 pounds before your ten-year high school reunion).

- A time when you told someone about a dream (e.g., that you wanted to take dance lessons). Did they cheer you on (e.g., "You can do it!") or discourage you (e.g., big eye roll)? Did you make it happen? How did it feel when you accomplished it?

- A time that you made an impact on someone else's life, and they told you about it (e.g., you came out to your parents, which helped a friend find the courage to come out, too, "thanks to you").

- A time when you made a challenging decision that required a new frame of mind (e.g., a move to a new city where you didn't know anyone but convinced yourself you'd make friends quickly, and did).

We are our own worst critics. Often, we look at the Rolodex of what we *haven't* accomplished. When we write down our accomplishments on paper, we see that we've done a lot to be proud of! Stand up. Raise your arms above your head. Look up into the sky and say, "Thank you. Thank you for show-ing me what I have accomplished in my life." Feels good, huh? Keep your "Rolodex" handy as you move through this book for motivation.

Become Your Own Best Friend

Don't you love to be around someone who you can spend hours on the phone with or have coffee with and just talk and talk and talk? Or what about when your best friend calls you and is upset, frustrated, and needs someone to listen? So you take some time to hear what they're saying and offer your best advice. You treat them with kindness, patience, and forgive-ness. You laugh, you cry—you even poke holes in their theories about why they can't possibly do the very thing they really want to do deep down inside.

Have you ever done that for yourself? I bet you treat the people near and dear to you with much more compassion and understanding than you've ever given yourself. I see this all the time in my coaching practice. It's why I often give my clients homework about learning to cultivate grace and compassion toward themselves. Now it's your turn:

Give yourself grace. It is okay if your website doesn't look exactly how you envisioned or your hair is a mess when you answer the door or your nail polish is chipped or any other number of things you want to be perfect but aren't. We all have chipped nails at some point.

Don't compare yourself to others. Would you compare your best friend to another friend to tell her how she can be better? I doubt it, so don't do that to yourself, either. While that woman who's sitting on the tip of the iceberg may seem like she's got it all, you have no idea what's going on under the water.

There is no right way to do anything. If you make a mistake, go back to square one, learn from your mistakes, and make the necessary corrections or changes.

Remember, you are just beginning this motivational journey to make a change in your life. The first step is to change your mindset so that motivation can take root and thrive! Start by being your own best friend.

Exercise: Learn from Past Choices

Simple daily habits like brushing your teeth and eating breakfast are part of a healthy life. Other positive habits you may have, such as meditating, knitting, or gardening, contribute to your sense of satisfaction and fulfillment. You're motivated to do those things, right? The key to making change or improving is to transfer that type of motivation to other areas of your life. But, if you aren't feeling motivated to make changes even though you're sure you really want to, there's probably something going on with you that is blocking your motivation. This next step is going to help you unpack those issues.

Fair warning: This exercise is not for the faint of heart. This call to action digs into past goals you didn't reach to figure out what happened to your motivation. Remember, it is okay that you didn't achieve them. Give yourself grace. However, you do need to figure out what happened. There could be many reasons you didn't accomplish your goals. Could it be due to a fear of failure, or even a fear of success?

Before we begin, I want you to practice "staying present." This exercise is called the 5-4-3-2-1 Mindfulness Exercise. It helps you stay on track if you start to feel overwhelmed. In fact, use this mindfulness exercise often to help ground yourself as you work through this book and beyond. For now, if anxiety starts to creep up while doing this exercise, take a moment to do the following:

1. Name five things you see.

2. Name four things you feel.

3. Name three things you can hear.

4. Name two things you can smell.

5. Name one thing you can taste.

Then take a deep breath and tell yourself, "I got this!" Okay, feeling centered? Grab your journal and go someplace where you won't be interrupted. Listen to soothing music, if you'd like. Read, reflect on, and respond to the following questions. I know there's a lot of them, but we're digging deep. Remember, I am in your stadium, cheering you on.

1. What was a goal you set for yourself but didn't see through?

2. How did you plan to achieve that goal? Did you have a plan or was it just an idea? Did you write it down in your journal? Did you ask someone to keep you accountable?

3. Did you take it day by day or was the goal task-oriented?

4. Did you subscribe to a reward system?

5. What motivated you in the beginning? Was it for yourself? For your family? Some other reason?

6. How long did this motivation last? Days, weeks, months, years?

7. When did it wane? After days, weeks, months, years?

8. Did you try to renew your motivation? What did that look like? Where did you get stuck?

9. What ultimately made you give up on the goal (e.g., failure, lack of time, frustrations)?

10. If you partially achieved your goal, what motivated you to get there?

11. Are you better at not succeeding than you are at succeeding?

12. Do you self-sabotage (#ouch)? Is it more comfortable to not push yourself to accomplish something than go for what you want?

13. What are the limiting factors (e.g., fear of failure, fear of the unknown, uncertainty, etc.) that held you back?

14. What was your reason for wanting to achieve the goal?

15. Do you feel guilty if you achieve success? Or do you feel that you don't deserve success?

16. Are you afraid you will be criticized for achieving or not achieving your goal?

17. Would you feel like a fraud or an impostor if you succeeded because you think you really don't know what you're talking about?

18. Do you put too much pressure on yourself to be perfect so you just give up?

19. Did the work feel so overwhelming that you said, "Peace out"?

20. Was the reward of accomplishing your goal not worth the effort?

How are you feeling? Are you overwhelmed? Are you pissed off at me? Want to throw this book in the garbage? That's okay. That's the point of this exercise. Finding out what is blocking you is one of the hardest parts of self motivation. You have to figure out *why* you are stuck. For now, simply be aware of your answers to these questions. You can repeat the exercise for different goals as well. This information will give you the insight you need to move forward, and you may want to refer to your answers from time to time as you work through the book, so keep your journal handy.

CHAPTER TWO

Setting the Stage

You'll have some hard conversations with yourself in this chapter, but you have nothing to fear. I've helped dozens of women take stock of their lives and instill life-altering changes they're still using today. I've seen the good, the bad, and the ugly, but the one constant I've discovered is that this journey is worth it. This chapter will help you set the course for your personal journey in all aspects of your life—from your physical and emotional health to your career and wealth to your personal relationships and spiritual practices.

What Motivates You?

This is a simple question, but it can be a tough one to answer. When I talk about motivation, I want to stick with the simple types of motivation, which are extrinsic and intrinsic. Extrinsic motivation encourages people from the outside (e.g., a shiny trophy, a new car, a high-salary job, or praise). Intrinsic motivation encourages people from within, such as a personal sense of accomplishment, that "hell yeah!" moment, or finding validation from yourself. Here are some scenarios to help you relate:

- A teen girl wants to audition for a big part in the school musical because she likes attention, but she was told she needed to improve her singing voice. She has the motivation to practice so that she can get the coveted role in the production. She's extrinsically motivated by praise from her classmates, parents, music teacher, the audience, etc.

- A woman who seemingly has everything—you know, 2.5 kids, the well-paying job, the beautiful house, and anything she wants—is in search of fulfillment outside her home and work. She once dreamed of being an artist in Paris, but let go of that idea when she started her career and became a wife and mother. Now, she's intrinsically motivated by a desire to express her artistic ability and signs up for an impressionist painting class at the museum.

- A stay-at-home mom has taken care of her kids and partner for the past 10 years. She's put on 20 pounds over the last two years. She doesn't feel good about herself and can't keep up with her kids. Her motivation to lose weight is both extrinsic and intrinsic: She wants to be healthier for her kids and wants to be healthier for herself physically and mentally.

While these scenarios are different, they show you what different motivations might look like. What about you? It can feel unnerving to search deep within yourself to find out what motivates you.

Exercise: Is Your Motivation Intrinsic, Extrinsic, or Both?

Grab your journal. Think about the scenarios in the previous section and answer the following questions:

- Even though your circumstances are different from those mentioned previously, which of the scenarios did you resonate with most: The teen who is extrinsically motivated by praise, the artist who is intrinsically motivated by self-expression, or the stay-at-home mom who is intrinsically and extrinsically motivated by being in better health for her kids and herself?

- Can you resonate with all three scenarios in different aspects of your life?

- Did any of these scenarios cause any anxiety or excitement when you read them? If so, which one(s) and why?

- What are you intrinsically motivated to do? What are you extrinsically motivated to do? What are you both intrinsically and extrinsically motivated to do?

Knowing where your motivation comes from is powerful insight as you work through this book to improve specific areas of your life.

Intentionality for the Win!

This book is framed on seven broad aspects of life that many coaches and therapists use to help their clients evaluate their choices: physical health and wellness, emotional health, personal relationships, creative endeavors, career and wealth, spiritual guidance, and community building. The choices you make in these seven different life realms are a testament to the things you value, desire, and strive for.

I see these aspects as interrelated, like two sides of the same coin. Yin and yang, if you will. I often notice that my clients who tend to crush one aspect of their life need to work on other aspects. For example, maybe you have fitness and nutrition down to a tee but need to work on your emotional health. Maybe you have a high-powered job that has brought you fame and fortune but your personal life isn't thriving. Perhaps your family life is rich with joy and satisfaction but your career has faltered.

Take another look at your Priority Pie (see page 9) and ask yourself where you excel and where you need help and support. I'm going to guess that you haven't figured *all* of them out. That's where this book comes into play. To be clear, I'm not saying you must excel at all of these aspects of life at the same time. What I am saying is that if you make time for each of these areas—when you can—you're on the right path to living your best life.

Let's take a closer look at each of these life aspects. In part two, I'll show you a variety of strategies to boost and maintain your self motivation in all of these areas.

PHYSICAL HEALTH AND WELLNESS

Sometimes this part of our life is neglected while we're trying to fit everything else in, but health and wellness is our most important commodity. Your physicality consists of your exercise routines and what you consume. Whether you are trying to lose those last five pounds to fit into your favorite jeans, trying to start an exercise routine, or simply wanting to prioritize a diet rich in whole foods, knowing what your body needs is essential.

But in a world where society is inundated with information about boosting and maintaining our health and wellness, it's easy to get discouraged. The onslaught is overwhelming, even for someone who has a master's in kinesiology, so please know that any discouragement you feel is understandable.

It's also good to think about your physical health beyond exercise and food. For example, regular visits to the doctor are a must, and then there's sleep. Sleep is absolutely crucial to the body, the brain, and the soul. It's the only time your cells get to rest, repair, and renew!

EMOTIONAL HEALTH

Your emotional health plays a significant role in your physical health, your relationships, and your career. Having the ability to regulate your emotions in a healthy way is crucial to your ability to successfully navigate life. In other words, your ability to deal with whatever life throws at you—both big and small—and not crumble into millions of pieces and shut down completely is the mark of an emotionally healthy person.

Maintaining healthy emotional resiliency is particularly challenging when your life is affected by things that are out of your control. For example, when I started to write this book, a pandemic was moving through the world. And when I finished this book, I went through a hurricane. Sure, that was likely a once-in-a-lifetime double whammy. But I do think it's fair to say that life's greatest challenges tend to exist in the minutiae of our days, for example: a car battery that doesn't start when you've got an important presentation at nine o'clock in the morning. Or, you've been really looking forward to a night out with your husband/partner, and your babysitter calls in sick.

All you want to do is cry or punch a wall or scream your head off, right? Which, on some occasions, may be the appropriate reaction. However, if life's daily trip-ups have you feeling completely defeated, your motivation will hit rock bottom in the blink of an eye. You must seek out methods to carry on as life comes at you, or it will simply walk all over you and you become a spectator at your very own sport.

PERSONAL RELATIONSHIPS

One of my favorite songs by The Beatles is "All You Need Is Love." The Fab Four were onto something. As humans, we need to be around other humans. Healthy personal relationships are essential for your happiness and well-being; they fuel your soul, that very essence of who you are and what you believe in. Studies show that positive, healthy personal relationships contribute to people living longer, being better at dealing with stress, being healthier overall, and feeling emotionally richer.

Family plays a massive role in adult relationships. Unfortunately, if your family relationships aren't ideal, or even toxic, they may influence what you expect from others. We all need to recognize that the quality of friendships versus the number of friendships is more important. Truly valuing and seeking out healthy relationships is a hallmark of maturity.

Having a healthy romantic relationship can also play a significant part in your life, especially when it's equally supported by love and growth. In a healthy relationship, you and your partner will flow with grace, appreciate each other, and be able to have both mundane *and* hard-core conversations without feeling personally attacked.

CREATIVE ENDEAVORS

Creativity is the human spirit's ability to express what it's feeling. Even if you can't draw a stick person, you *do* have a creative side. Maybe you like dancing in the kitchen to your favorite music (like me) or are an amazing baker who rivals the Cake Boss. I mean, if hanging wallpaper without a crease in sight is your jam, who am I to judge? Creativity takes many different forms. As kids we are all considered creative. We play make-believe, draw pictures, build with blocks, etc. But as adults, we tend to abandon the creative outlets we cherished as young kids or teens because we've got car payments and other things to take care of. I mean, who has time to even think about finding the time?

You do.

Here's an example: I have a friend, Stefanie an athlete and the mom of two boys, who found her creative outlet running an athletic clothing company Tri Sirena Apparel. She also had skin cancer. Her company produces athletic clothes with the UPF built in. To promote her business, she posts videos on social media of herself dancing while she's wearing her clothes. Learning to embrace your creative side like she did—whether it's dancing in your bedroom, singing in the shower, or showing the world your moves on social media—will undoubtedly bring you joy and a sense of accomplishment.

CAREER AND WEALTH

As much as we want to think otherwise, what we do for a living defines who we are to society. Say the words "construction worker," "waitress," "accountant," "nurse," "stay-at-home mom," "horse trainer," *and* "sculptor," and I guarantee you have conjured up visions in your mind and even have a slight idea of the lifestyle each person lives based on their assumed income or wealth. We all do this. And that's fine. Are you satisfied with how your particular role defines you? Or are you looking for the motivation to make a change? Do you want to pursue a different career path, make more money, or cut back the hours you devote to business?

While others may see us for *what* we do, how we define wealth is up to us. Perhaps your mid-income job allows you time to pursue your passions in the evenings. Or maybe you are a high-salary executive who works all hours of the day and into the evenings, and that's where you want to be. Your wealth is not only monetary but also the experiences you gain.

When I worked as a marine mammal trainer, I worked really long hours and lots of weekends. I was up early and always wet. But the job provided me a wealth of extraordinary experiences. I eventually got out of that line of work because the payoff wasn't working for me anymore. Starting my coaching business wasn't a slam dunk right away. There were some lean years, but I was also very fulfilled. My career now, as a life coach, is how the world sees me, but my wealth is partly in monetary compensation and partly what I take away from the experiences of empowering all women to harness their inner strength and find freedom through change.

SPIRITUAL GUIDANCE

Spirituality is an individual choice. People are drawn to what works for them—going to a place of worship, the power of prayer, meditation, visualizations, dreams, ceremonies, or talking to a higher power only right before bed. I saw spirituality best described in a 2011 online article by Larry Culliford in *Psychology Today*: "Spirituality is like an adventure park waiting to be explored." You can decide to ride the daring roller coaster and be adventurous or sit on a bench to watch everyone else.

Photographer Ansel Adams's form of spirituality was nature. For the Pope, it's the Almighty. For others, it's the Universe. I tend to blend a few things, but when I need advice or help, I ask for it and I *look* for it. For example, if I see a butterfly, I know I am on the right path. Whatever you choose for your spiritual path is the right path for you. Don't let anyone tell you differently.

People's faith can be tested every day. Finding ways to strengthen your faith in humankind, in a power that defies logic, can assist you in other areas of your life. It isn't always an easy path to take, but when you do take it, the reward can be an awakening that can feed your soul for a lifetime.

SUPPORTING COMMUNITY

I define community as a feeling of fellowship with others as a result of sharing common attitudes, interests, and goals. So many communities and people are coming together these days in so many ways, such as standing for a cause, becoming a part of a group, or giving back in ways that are not self-serving. For example, many have come forward to support the Black Lives Matter movement, but this movement, as well as others, highlights the need for us to do more as a whole so that we can all enjoy equal rights and basic human dignities. The movement for women's empowerment has been gaining strides, but there is still much more for us to do to protect our rights. The chapter devoted to this topic is close to my heart because we all need a tribe or a community to guide us, help us grow, and stand next to us in our journey called life.

Exercise: Set Your Goals

Pull out your journal and get out your art supplies, because it's time to set your goals. In this exercise, you're going to develop a statement and visual representation of what you want your life to be like and become. Ask yourself where you want to thrive in your life and what you want to do to motivate yourself to achieve that.

This is the crux of who you are and who you strive to be. Think of it as the filling of your Priority Pie. You'll look at it every day to keep yourself motivated. My life statement, "I have been reborn, physically, mentally, and spiritually," is on my calendar and my vision board, and I look at it every day as a reminder of where I want to go and who I want to become.

I encourage you to do both parts A and B of this exercise. By the way, it's okay to adjust your goals when your priorities change, and you will notice that your motivation can change as well. You can revisit this exercise whenever you feel the need.

PART A: WRITE IT DOWN

Putting your thoughts on paper is one of the best ways to keep yourself accountable. Seeing your ideas and goals in front of you means you can't ignore them. Write down your statement, highlighting your goals and dreams. Be as specific as possible. For example:

- I want a job that pays enough for me to live comfortably that involves working from home and having time to spend with my family in the evenings.

- I want to spend more time on my creative passion, which means I will shut my work, computer, and phone down from 7:00 p.m. to 7:00 a.m. Work will always be there.

- I want to cross the finish line of my first marathon when I am 40 years old. I will hire a coach, clean up my nutrition, and start strength training by the end of August, and do my first marathon in February.

If you'd prefer, you can record your statement via voice memo or even video record it. Play back the recording to remind yourself of your goal(s) often. In fact, you might choose to do this for all the writing prompts in this book. It's up to you. You may also choose to write and record. Sometimes when I'm out running and I have a fantastic idea, I will pull out my phone and record my thoughts on the go.

PART B: CREATE A VISION BOARD

Oh, vision boards, I love you so! Collecting images of your goals, dreams, and ideas in a visual format that expresses what you want your life to be like is one powerful tool. Athletes use this strategy all the time to motivate themselves, but so do people who are looking for change in any area of life.

I don't have a lot of things I insist of my clients, but I do insist they create a vision board and organize it in a way that speaks to their personal and professional goals. I also instruct them to have an "other goals" category. An example of that would be a new house. Then, they would fill the board with how they would want that house to look, for example: three bedrooms, two baths, office space, patio, etc.

You can go the old-fashioned way, scouring magazines and newspapers for images, words, and quotes, and then cut and glue them onto a poster or corkboard. Another way is to do it online. Pinterest is a well-known online platform for vison boards. I personally like the websites Canva and PicMonkey, which have vision-board templates and free images. You can always grab pictures from search engines as well.

Once you've created your vision board, use it as a motivational tool by looking at it daily to get you where you want to go. I recommend you do a vision board for each aspect of your life.

Your Motivational Tool Kit

So far, you've looked at your priorities. You've also analyzed past choices and what worked and what didn't. I know that probably wasn't super fun, but it was necessary. You recognized that you want to make a change in your life, and it will take time, but look at what you have accomplished already:

- You've realized you are stronger than you think.

- You've written down your goals and created a vision board.

- You've set out on a mission!

These necessary tasks are all foundational to set you up for success so you can begin creating your plan for change. Up next is a closer look at how to use the different tips, tools, and strategies to help you achieve your goals and stay motivated during easy times *and* tough times.

BUILD-ONS AND ONE-OFFS

The way we think, act, and feel is unique to each of us. You may find that certain strategies resonate with you while others either don't or need to be tweaked to keep you engaged. For example, when you were tasked with doing a vision board, you may have chosen to create it virtually if you didn't want to spend time literally cutting and pasting. As you get down and dirty with making a change for yourself, you'll find many strategies to try throughout this book. Do what works for you and what will help you personally stay motivated and on the course you've set out for yourself. For example, in the chapter on health and wellness, you'll see it isn't just about working out. I will discuss types of fitness, nutrition, sleep, being happy, mindset, and more. You can pick and choose what you want to work on or try them all out to see which ones work best for you.

You'll also notice that some of the exercises and strategies build upon one another, while others require just a single action item. For example, when you learn a mindfulness technique, you'll want to incorporate it into your daily practices. In other cases, it's just a onetime thing for the insight it gives you as you continue on your journey.

You may also realize that some of these strategies don't work for you at all. You might have your own method to your madness. Good, stick with it. Don't break what isn't broken. Just figure out what you need. For example, if you don't need to focus on your health, motivate yourself to focus on your emotional state or vice versa.

ACTION ITEMS

You can read all you want about self-help and self-improvement. But if you are not going to do anything to move forward, then what's the point? This book doesn't want to sit on a bookshelf and collect dust. This book is about action. It's intended to be read, marked up, drawn in, underlined, high-lighted, shared, and used to help you achieve your goals.

You've already started to journal and dabble in mindfulness. You can expect more of those techniques, plus many others: five-year planning; checklists; daily reminders, and so much more. This book is here for you to reevaluate your life. I know you want to make change happen, so let's do something about it. I can't wait to hear about your results!

MINDFULNESS

The practice of mindfulness helps you observe life as it is happening. Yes, that is hard to achieve, particularly in today's world. But honestly, it is one of the best tricks to have in your tool kit.

As you take this journey, mindfulness can provide clarity and help reduce stress during these changes. Maybe you are in a challenging situation with a business partner, so instead of focusing on the future, focus on making changes to improve your relationship. Another is finding out that a dear friend has cancer. Instead of instantly imagining the worst, mindfully take 10 minutes to meditate and pray for your friend's recovery.

Being mindful is a constant struggle for me. I love to control things and plan, plan, plan. It's something that I am working on. If you're an old pro at mindfulness, great. If not, I want you to take five minutes right now. Head outside, smell the fresh air, and walk barefoot in the grass. Look up. What do you see? What do you feel? On page 67, you'll find a simple mindfulness practice you can use throughout this book (and beyond) to ground yourself and help clear your mind whenever you need to refocus.

REFRAMING

A few years ago, I was teaching my niece, Taryn, how to ride her bike. She was all in—for about 30 minutes. That's when she turned to me and said, "Aunt Jennifer, I can't do this. Riding a bike is so hard. I don't want to fall." Taryn was succumbing to those internal monologues we all experience, which tell us that a task or endeavor we are trying to accomplish is too hard, we simply can't do it, and it's not worth the effort.

It can be hard as hell to get out of that mindset of "I can't." For example, you are 15 minutes into your acoustic guitar lessons on YouTube and you're already discouraged, saying things such as, "This is really hard; I'm not sure I can make it through the entire hour-long session." Reframing your thoughts is about recognizing when you mentally beat yourself up, talk yourself out of something, or merely push away your desire. And then—and this is the most important part—alter what you're telling yourself by using more encouraging and positive language. Reframing the guitar lesson would be saying, "Wow! I've already learned one chord! That means I can probably learn four chords by the time this lesson is over!"

See the difference?

By the way, after a pep talk and assurances that her helmet, elbow pads, and kneepads would protect her from injury if she did fall, Taryn got out of her own way and told herself that she could do it—and she learned how to ride a bike. Afterward, we went to the Apple store to get her earbuds. Yes, I used extrinsic motivation to help my niece learn to ride a bike. And guess what, you can reward yourself for little successes to help yourself stay motivated! Reframing and rewarding yourself are powerful motivations!

Feeling Overwhelmed?

When you feel overwhelmed, what you're really feeling is stress, which we all handle differently. Some people charge forward, into the fire. Others want to get into bed and throw the covers over their head. I'm not sure either way is the best way. Pressure can be a good thing if you know how to handle it. First, if something is triggering you, you need to figure out what it is, and then you need to figure out how to respond to the stressor.

What is causing you to feel overwhelmed or stressed? Can you take 10 minutes for yourself and go back to what is stressing you after you've had some "me" time? Can it wait until later or tomorrow? Can you wake up 30 minutes earlier for some personal time so you can start the day feeling calm? Can you head to your bedroom 30 minutes before bedtime for some "me" time, so you can go to sleep feeling calm? These are all important questions to ask yourself to start reducing feelings of stress and responding to the things you may find overwhelming with a little more mindfulness.

Now, here's the big question: Does the idea of making a change feel overwhelming? If your answer is yes, I have two affirmations you can use to get past that type of stress: "I deserve to make a change for myself" and "I will make this change for myself."

If you need support to reduce the stress in your life, don't hesitate to ask for it. You can turn to friends, family, or colleagues, and you can also join a community or support group. In that case, you can add another affirmation: "I have a fantastic community supporting me in making a change." (And if you don't, I got you! Join my community on Facebook: Monarch Mindset Squad!) You have always had your wings—now it's time to fly.

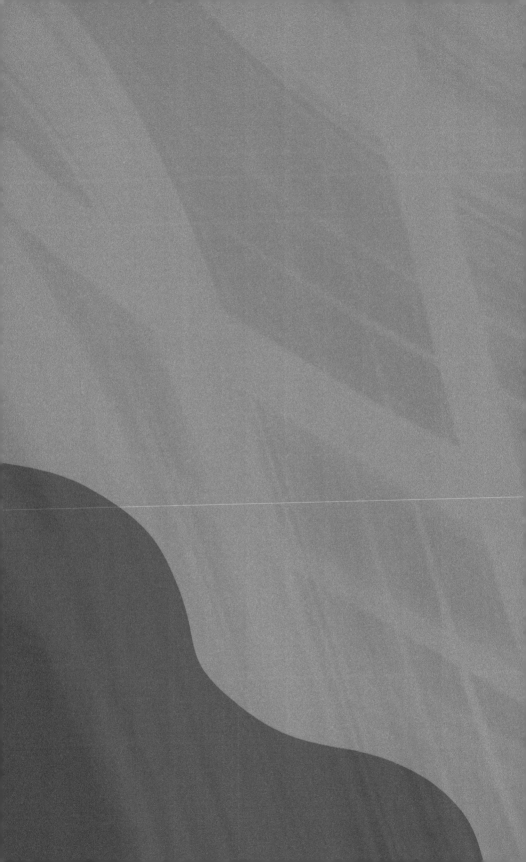

Doing the Work

CHAPTER THREE

You Don't Have to Run a Marathon, but Get Active

Health and Wellness

In this chapter, you'll look at your physical health and wellness routine—exercise, nutrition, the importance of sleep, being happy, your mindset, and being still. Within those topics, I'll offer a wide swath of how-to tips, strategies, and techniques to get you motivated to make important changes for the better around these issues and how to reach your goals, whatever they may be. As you begin, here's an important question to keep in mind: What does improving health and wellness in your life mean to you? Think beyond losing weight, feeling fit, or "looking good." Dive deep into your core about what being healthy means to you.

When I was coaching a strength and conditioning class, I'd often see a mix of people of varying abilities. One of the basic exercises was a pull-up. One young client, Melissa, was a super-athletic runner, but she could not do a pull-up to save her life. She became frustrated and decided to set a goal to successfully do pull-ups by the end of summer. She was intrinsically motivated by a desire to have the upper-body strength to improve her physique overall.

Over the course of many weeks, we worked on a plan to develop her muscles that would propel her to a pull-up. After each CrossFit class, I'd have her engage in a variety of specific strength-building exercises. About two months in, Melissa still could not do a pull-up. Being athletic her entire life, it was hard for her to see herself not achieve a fitness goal. "Take a couple of days off from practicing," I told her. "Let the body recover and come back in a few days."

When Melissa came back to class, she had a look of determination in her eyes. After our warm-up, she went to the pull-up bar and knocked it out. It was mid-August. She had achieved her goal with weeks to spare! When I asked her what had made the difference, she told me that she had stopped obsessing about it and just let her muscles do the work.

I know that CrossFit isn't for everyone. However, I make the case that Melissa's process to finally complete a proper pull-up will apply the same to you. She set a goal, developed a plan to stay motivated, stopped obsessing over it, and found her determination.

You Are What You Eat

The goal of eating properly is to improve and/or maintain your health to live a long and prosperous life. What better motivation could there be? Eating a whole-food, plant-based diet—or at least a minimal reliance on meat—is the best path forward. Whole foods such as fruits, vegetables, nuts, seeds, beans, milk and some dairy, eggs, meat, poultry, seafood, and limited processed foods are your best bets here. The idea is to know beforehand what the best choices are, as many people can make the wrong choices if they wait until they are hungry. Planning your meals can help you get in a routine, making your daily tasks more manageable and staying on track with your body and your mind.

Let's look now at some foods that are good for your brain health, as well as the macronutrients and micronutrients your body needs to function at its best. Not only will your brain and body be in optimal condition, but you'll also have the energy you need to sustain your motivation for other things you'd like to accomplish.

FOOD FOR FOCUS

According to the *Journal of the American Society on Aging*, the human brain is quite active. It uses about 20 to 30 percent of a person's energy at rest. Imagine how much it uses when it's trying to work out a problem! So, if you are trying to function at work or school, the right food can play a significant role in motivation.

Here are just five types of food that are good for brain health to start including in your diet:

- Fatty fish (such as salmon, anchovies, mackerel, and tuna)

- Walnuts

- Chia seeds

- Edamame

- Greek yogurt

Your goal this week is to commit to eating at least one brain-boosting food each day. For example, use Greek yogurt in place of mayonnaise or sour cream in your tuna salad. (My favorite lunch is chopping up a rotisserie chicken, mixing it with Greek yogurt, and adding some chopped walnuts and green apples. Then, I scoop it up with whole-grain crackers.) You can add crushed walnuts to your salads, add chia seeds to your smoothies, and snack on edamame. Take time to learn what other foods are good for brain health, too!

THINK BIG—MACRONUTRIENTS

A common saying among personal trainers is "Abs aren't made in the gym but in the kitchen." What that means is what you eat is as equally important as exercise. Pledging to have a balanced diet is one thing, sticking to it is another. A better understanding of the basic components of nutrition, can motivate you to maintain a well-balanced, healthy diet.

Macronutrients (carbohydrates, proteins, and fats) are the central part of your diet. According to the *NSCA's Guide to Sport and Exercise Nutrition*, carbohydrates and fats are the primary nutrients used for energy production, while protein contributes a small amount.

Here are some good choices to focus on when it comes to macronutrients:

- Carbohydrates: whole grains, rice, vegetables, and fruits and berries

- Fats: avocados, olive oil, olives, walnuts, chia seeds, nuts, fatty beef, fatty fish

- Protein: meats, poultry, eggs, cheese, quinoa, nuts, fish, tofu, soy, and animal by-products

When it comes to figuring out how many macronutrients you need to consume, there is not much of a secret sauce. There are plenty of calculators online, but this is what you will need to know for that calculator: age, height, weight, activity level at work, how often you work out, and how intense your workouts are. Need a calculator? Here are a couple:

- My website: JenRulon.com/macro-counting

- IIFYM (If It Fits Your Macros): IIFYM.com/iifym-calculator

THINK LITTLE—MICRONUTRIENTS

If macronutrients are the key to building the body and brain, then micronutrients are the key to sustaining body and brain health. Micronutrients are the vitamins and minerals you consume when you eat. They are essential for the overall health of your immune system. According to the World Health Organization, "Micronutrient deficiencies can cause visible and dangerous health conditions, but they can also lead to less clinically notable reductions in energy level, mental clarity, and overall capacity."

Here are some of the best sources to get your micronutrients:

- Vitamin B6: chicken, bananas, potatoes with skin, pork loin

- Vitamin C: citrus fruits, tomatoes, broccoli

- Vitamin E: almonds, peanut butter, sunflower seeds

- Calcium: milk, cheese and other dairy foods, leafy greens and vegetables such as kale and spinach, calcium-fortified soy drinks

- Magnesium: whole wheat, nuts, seeds

- Zinc: oysters, crab, dark turkey meat

If you are young and healthy and eat a well-balanced diet that's rich in whole foods, you are likely getting your requirements of nutrients. If you aren't sure or if you are older or have specific health issues, go to your doctor for a blood test; they will help provide what you are deficient in and offer a multivitamin or mineral if needed.

You Are What You Drink

According to the *NSCA's Guide to Sport and Exercise Nutrition*, water makes up about 60 percent of an average person's body weight. One of the many things I learned when I was studying for my master's is that when it comes to fluids, the human body's thirst mechanism is a little slow. By the time your brain realizes it's thirsty, you're already dehydrated. And when you're dehydrated, you're likely to lose focus, consume more sugar, and feel more agitated. The next time you have a headache, ask yourself if you've had any water today.

The best way to stay ahead of dehydration is to count your water intake. According to the Mayo Clinic, women should drink about 2.7 liters of water a day. Environment, activity levels, age, pregnancy, and overall health play a factor, so if you're unsure how much to drink, ask your doctor. Once you know, track it to make sure you get enough. Here's how:

Manual tracking: Get yourself a one-liter bottle and break down your day. Drink a bottle before noon. Drink another bottle before five o'clock. And drink the rest of your daily intake in the early evening.

App tracking: Yes, you can download an app to track your water intake. Here are a couple: Hydro Coach, WaterMinder, and Aqualert. Check out your app store to see what's available.

WATCH YOUR INTAKE OF SODA, ALCOHOL, AND JUICES

We humans just love our soda, alcohol, juices, and coffee. So what's the problem? Regular sodas have empty calories, and diet sodas have artificial sweeteners—neither of which are ideal for health and wellness. If you are a big soda drinker, it's time to think about switching to sparkling water.

With regard to alcohol, this can be a touchy subject for some, as alcohol abuse can play a detrimental role not only in your life but in others' lives. According to the National Institute on Alcohol Abuse and Alcoholism, a standard drink is considered 12 ounces of beer, 5 ounces of wine, or 1.5 ounces of distilled spirits. However, it's not uncommon for people to have more than one "standard" drink. And while juicing can be a great way to get your recommended serving of fruits and veggies, too much juice equals too much sugar. (I'll talk about coffee, specifically, in just a moment.)

Keeping your soda, juice, and alcohol consumption to a reasonable amount is important to an overall healthy lifestyle. I have three easy tips to help you make good on that charge:

1. Don't keep juice, alcohol, or soda in the house. Make it a treat when you go out for breakfast or dinner.

2. Count your drinks per week. How many times did you head to the juice bar? How often are you going out for drinks or fixing cocktails at home?

3. Do something else. Meet friends for a hike instead of drinks. Grab sparkling water instead of grabbing a soda. Drink more water with some lemon in it instead of high-calorie juice.

As with everything, it is all about moderation and enjoying the moments with a glass of champagne, perhaps, to celebrate your new job or dropping those last five pounds!

LIFE HAPPENS—COFFEE HELPS

"A bad day with coffee is better than a good day without it." That's just a joke, but there's something to it: Studies have shown that doses of four mg/kg of caffeine can increase mental alertness and improve logical reasoning, according to *NSCA's Guide to Sport and Exercise Nutrition*. But how much caffeine is too much? According to the Mayo Clinic, up to 400 milligrams of caffeine a day appears to be safe, which is about four cups of brewed coffee. But coffee isn't the only beverage with caffeine: It's also found in soda and "energy shot" drinks.

To get a better handle on your caffeine consumption, ask yourself:

• Are you jittery?

• Are you getting headaches?

• Are you dealing with anxiety or anxious thoughts?

• Does drinking coffee late in the day affect your sleep habits?

If you answered yes to any of those questions, it's time to pull back. How? The first step is to stop drinking caffeine in the evening. I make every effort to clean up my coffeepot and put away any remnants of it so I don't brew late in the day. If you like the idea of a warm cup of something in the evening, switch to herbal tea.

Get Your Heart Rate Up

To motivate yourself to get your heart rate up, which exercises and strengthens your cardiac muscle, figure out what *you* love to do and how you can get your beautiful body to move! Long story short, according to the current guidelines from HHS.gov, you should move your body 150 to 300 minutes a week with exercise. Which means you would be exercising approximately 20 to 40 minutes a day.

Here are a few 30-minute exercise routines to choose from to motivate you to create a routine that works for you and makes you want to work out longer:

- Move your body by walking, dancing, cycling, etc., for 15 minutes. Then, do 3 rounds of 5 push-ups (on your knees or against the wall), followed by 10 air squats (use a chair or a box, if you need to), and then 15 sit-ups (or a 30-second plank hold).

- Download a walking app and track 1,000 steps, which should take about 15 to 20 minutes. Grab some water. Spend the next 15 minutes stretching or doing yoga. If you need a 15-minute stretching or yoga routine, you'll find a ton on YouTube.

- Walk or run 5 minutes from home and then 5 minutes back. Using indoor mats or working on a flat outdoor surface, spend 10 minutes doing as many rounds as you can of the following: 20 walking lunges (10 each leg), 15 sit-ups, or a 1-minute plank on elbows or hands (if necessary, go as long as you can, rest, and try again until you get to a minute). For the last 10 minutes, walk or run 5 minutes from home and then 5 minutes back.

Remember, the goal of getting your body moving is to start to feel better. When you start feeling better, you will be motivated to keep improving!

BUILD YOUR ENGINE

I have helped many triathletes cross the finish line with a smile on their face, but their journey didn't occur overnight, nor will your journey to becoming healthier. When I get athletes ready for a race, the very first thing I try to do is help them build their "engine" or aerobic capacity.

Aerobic training means training "with oxygen" for an extended period. Swimming, cycling, running, dancing, walking, or otherwise moving for 30 minutes a day, five days a week with moderate intensity will improve blood flow to the heart and provide energy to many parts of your body, such as your muscles, nerves, and brain.

Building capacity is how you can endure longer periods of exercise and reap the benefits: weight loss and reduced blood sugar. It won't happen overnight, but if you keep at it for at least three weeks straight, you'll start to see a difference. As you put together your engine plan, consider the following:

- How do you want to move your body?

- What type of movement challenges your soul?

- What physical activities make you smile?

For me, it's running. But you could also salsa dance, ride your bike, roller-skate, surf, even walk. Just make sure to spend 30 minutes a day doing it.

THE NEED FOR SPEED

Once you've built your engine, it's time to build speed, also known as anaerobic training. Anaerobic training means training "without oxygen," which is a little confusing. It means that you utilize your stored energy resources (carbohydrates/glucose) first during the training rather than oxygen itself.

Examples of anaerobic training include a burst of sprinting, jumping, weight lifting, or anything that has a short duration and high-intensity movements. I am a big fan of Tabata Intervals. They were created in the late nineties by Irisawa Koichi, the head coach of the Japanese Olympic speed skating team. Essentially, a Tabata Interval looks like this:

- 20 seconds of all-out exercise effort

- 10 seconds of rest

- Repeating for eight cycles or a total of four minutes

Here are some specific examples of Tabata you can try at home once you've built your engine:

- Lower body movements, such as squats, lunges or dumbbell squats for 20 seconds all-out, followed by a 10-second rest. Repeat eight cycles.

- Upper body movements, such as push-ups and dips, for 20 seconds all-out, followed by a 10-second rest. Repeat eight cycles.

- Cardio movements, such as burpees, mountain climbers, a run or walk, for 20 seconds all-out, followed by a 10-second rest. Repeat eight cycles.

THE PERFECT STORM

The perfect storm is a combination of aerobic and anaerobic movement that will help you achieve your fitness goals. When you train in the aerobic state, you will burn carbohydrates and fats. When you train in an anaerobic state, you will burn carbohydrates. But if you start focusing on aerobic and anaerobic exercises, your body will begin to burn fats and carbohydrates at an equal rate.

So, how do you create the perfect storm? Take these actions:

1. Grab your calendar and color-code your workouts.

2. Block out five 30-minute sessions each day for your workout.

3. Start with 30 minutes of cardio. You can even break it up. Do 15 minutes in the morning and 15 minutes in the afternoon. Plan on doing this for four weeks to build your engine.

4. Once you've started building your engine and feeling more comfortable, replace one of the cardio workouts with a speed-building workout. Plan to do this for at least three weeks.

5. Getting even more comfortable? Add another speed-building workout. Now you are at two speed-building workouts and three cardio workouts.

6. Build on that until you've reached your personal perfect storm.

Are you interested in more workouts? Shoot me an email at jen@jenrulon. com, and I will send you my top 10 at-home workouts to help you maintain that drive!

Stop Fighting Bedtime

You hear it all the time—sleep is crucial for success. According to the journal *Sleep and Breathing,* rest is an "essential biological function with major roles in recovery, energy conservation, and survival." Sleep also plays a role in metabolic regulation, emotional regulation, athletic performance, memory connection, brain recovery, and learning.

Humans spend one-third of their lives asleep. But in the past 20 to 30 years, the number of hours people sleep has declined due to work, commuting, and using our phones, computers, and televisions.

So how much sleep is enough? The average adult needs seven to eight hours a night, but more than 35 percent of adults are getting less than seven hours, according to the CDC.

Here are three motivational tips that can help you get a better night's sleep:

- Shut down your phone 30 minutes before you get into bed. You laugh. Yes, put your phone in the kitchen or your office. Grab a *real* clock to use as an alarm.

- Read a book in bed. A good old-fashioned one made of paper or an e-reader with a blue light should work.

- Have sex in bed: Need I say more?

THE MENTAL BENEFITS OF SLEEP

Our brain is highly complex and needs tender loving care every day. A good night's sleep with rapid eye movement (REM) clears toxins and waste products from your brain and boosts cell renewal. That's why a lack of sleep can negatively affect cognition and alertness. The danger of this is no more apparent than driving while tired.

Your mind may keep you awake thinking about all the events of the day and your to-do list for tomorrow, so it's a good idea to prepare your mind to sleep. I do a meditation before bed to prepare my mind. (You can find sleep meditations on YouTube.) You can also use a sleep mantra, such as "My mind needs only to rest right now" and repeat it until you fall asleep. Many people tend to fall asleep well before they get to 100 repetitions.

When you take these steps to prepare your mind for sleep, you will be in a better place mentally, with sleep in your back pocket. This will help you make better decisions and be more motivated, happier, and smarter the next day.

THE PHYSICAL BENEFITS OF SLEEP

Sleep plays a role in the organs, tissues, and muscles in our bodies, not just our brains. According to a 2015 study published in the *Annual Review of Public Health*, a lack of sleep is one of most significant risk factors of cardio-vascular health, which is the number-one cause of death in adults. The same study showed that children who are considered short sleepers (under seven hours) were 55 percent more likely to be obese.

Here are some ways to focus on sleep if you aren't getting enough:

- Add 10 minutes to your bedtime. For example, if you usually head to bed at 10:30 p.m., getting into bed by 10:20 p.m. can help your flow of getting more sleep.

- Avoid exercising about two to three hours before you head to bed.

- Make your bedroom cool and dark. It may be difficult to get comfortable if you feel warm or if light is keeping you awake.

TRACK YOUR SLEEP

When I was training for the Ironman in Hawaii, I started using a sleep app. I quickly learned I wasn't getting sufficient sleep. I would wake up in the middle of the night several times, and my deep sleep was less than it should have been. And guess what. My training on those days was in the gutter. What did I do? I worked on getting better sleep.

Whether or not you are an athlete, here are a few devices that can help you track your sleep to figure out if you need more:

- WHOOP is a sleep-monitoring device that will help you track the hours you sleep and get into better sleeping habits.

- Fitbit devices can track not only your movement and heart rate but also your sleep.

- Sleep Genius—This technology is used by NASA to help astronauts sleep better.

You Be You

It is time to consider your mindset. I'll discuss this topic more in chapter 4, but let's dabble a bit here. Your mindset is the established set of attitudes held by you. There are two types of mindsets, fixed and growth. People with fixed mindsets think that their qualities are inborn and unchangeable. Examples include statements such as, "I am either good at it or I am not," "When I am frustrated, I give up," or "Ugh, let me just stick to what I know!" People with a growth mindset, on the other hand, believe that their qualities can be developed by commitment and hard work. Example statements include, "Challenges help me grow," "I like to try new things," and "I am good with change."

Since you're reading this book, it's likely you have a growth mindset and just need a little motivation and encouragement to get unstuck. To learn more about mindset, visit verywellmind.com and read "Why Mindset Matters for Your Success." I know that you know you are perfectly capable of making change! And, if you identify with a fixed mindset, the motivation strategies in this book can help you break free. Let's discuss two ways to break free now.

STOP COMPARING YOURSELF TO OTHERS

How often have you looked at someone or something on social media and said, "Wow, that woman is in shape. I want to look like that!" or "That is a beautiful house!" or "They have a perfect life!" Some of this is normal, but when it starts consuming you, it is time to reevaluate your world.

When you compare yourselves to others, it can deprive you of your joy. You are so focused on what they did, how they did it, etc., that you are not focusing on yourself. One of the best ways to combat the comparison habit is to recognize your wins in your own life, big or small.

Did you wake up today? That is a win!

Did you make the bed, shower, get dressed, get the kids off to school, go to work, make dinner for the family, etc.? So many wins there!

Small wins are wins. Recognizing the little victories will help you realize that you are enough!

CONTROL WHAT YOU CAN CONTROL

One of the best pieces of advice I've received was from my own triathlon coach, Brandon Marsh, who said, "Control what you can control." When I was training for my Ironman Triathlon races, I was focused on myself for the most part. There were moments that I started worrying about the weather, who was going to show up on race day, or how I was going to beat this or that athlete. I was spending so much energy worrying about people or the environment that I couldn't control that I was wasting energy where it didn't serve me.

There are a lot of things you cannot control, such as the weather, your coworker's attitude, a gossiping friend, etc. When you start to worry about all of the things that are out of your realm, try these five strategies to help you reset and push out the anxiety:

1. Focus on your mindset. Reframing negative thoughts brings to mind what you are grateful for.

2. Focus on your work ethic. Whatever you do, make every effort to be the best at it.

3. Focus on how you treat others. Being kind and considerate is truly the best practice.

4. Focus on your health and wellness. Be sure you're taking care of your physical, mental, and emotional needs.

5. Focus on the language you use. Carefully choosing your words when talking to a friend, coworker, or partner makes a lasting impression.

The Art of Being Still

The key to stillness is to have intention behind it. The goal of being still is to help clear your mind, live your best life, and stay motivated when the world may not be handing you puppies and kittens. Here's one way to practice stillness:

1. Schedule a time, such as at six o'clock, every morning, before others in your household get up.

2. Find a place in your home where you will not be interrupted.

3. Set a timer for 5 to 30 minutes. (It's up to you how long to practice. Start by giving yourself grace.)

4. Relax and quiet your mind by thinking of yourself floating in a bright blue sky. As you are floating, you pass through a cloud. Those "clouds" are your thoughts, and they will always be there. Acknowledge those thoughts and continue floating on by.

5. Do this until your timer goes off. Take a deep breath and move on with your day.

STEP AWAY FROM YOUR DEVICE

How often is someone talking with you and you are distracted by the phone or computer? Remember those good old-fashioned conversations we used to have with each other? How often do you check your phone one last time before you jump into bed? How many times have you grabbed your phone when you are trying to clean the house? Or trying to study, and the computer is chiming in with emails? Productivity and learning decrease, and we're no longer present in the moment because we are losing our focus to digital distractions.

To find the stillness that is present in every moment, put your phone in another room, turn it off, or put it on airplane mode.

Taking a rest from your devices helps you stay present, improves your sleep, and helps you achieve the goals you want to achieve.

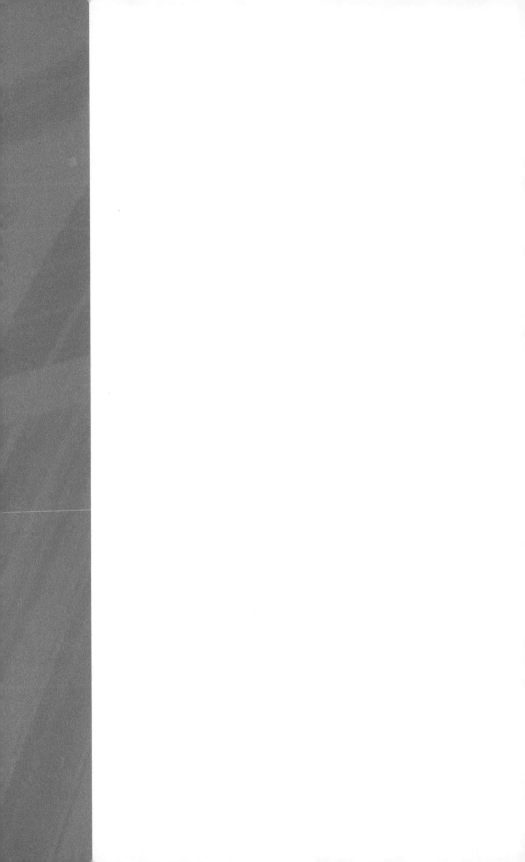

CHAPTER FOUR

Emotional Resilience Is More Than Feelings

Emotional Health

Some of us are our own worst enemies when it comes to our emotional health. We encourage and support our girlfriends, family, and kids (if we have them), but then we forget to take care of ourselves and our emotional headspace. In this chapter, you'll learn motivational strategies to improve your emotional resilience. This includes letting go, finding forgiveness, learning how to stop self-sabotaging, increasing your self-awareness, and finding your purpose.

MEET LESLIE

Leslie has been a successful social media entrepreneur for nearly four years. Because of the success of her marketing agency, her education and expertise about the medium are valuable. However, when I met Leslie, her self-esteem had taken a big dive. A disgruntled follower was bullying her in the comments section of Leslie's social media account, and she was starting to lose faith in her expertise. During our initial meeting, I asked Leslie what she believed was her most limiting factor. She responded that perfectionism was her greatest detriment. Leslie's "perfect" record had been derailed by the follower's rude comments, and her emotional resiliency needed a boost.

For three months, Leslie and I talked weekly to discuss issues in her business, personal life, and everything in between. It became apparent that many of her struggles revolved around staying organized and having a structure in her work life. I knew that setting specific goals each week would give her a sense of accomplishment. Calls to action were effective for her because she liked being held accountable when we'd check in each week.

As our relationship continued, our conversations steered toward her personal life. Leslie admitted that her self-doubt thwarted any real achievements she set her sights on for a given day. A morning routine that consisted of walking the dog, making breakfast for her and her partner, and clarifying her non-negotiables for the day kept her motivated and focused. After a few weeks, the strategies we created to keep her motivated and accountable were paying off. Leslie's confidence grew each week because she could see firsthand that her goals were being achieved. It also helped her let go of the fear of not being perfect. Her self-esteem started to increase in her personal relationships as well. Of course, we are all different, but here are the steps that helped Leslie build her emotional resilience:

1. Recognize your boundaries. (I get detailed about boundaries in chapter 5.)
2. Get into a morning routine.

3. Set up the non-negotiables in your life (work, kids, working out, meditating, quiet time, etc.).
4. Set aside time for rest, which is crucial for emotional health.
5. Find an accountability buddy.

Leslie's transformation from doubting herself to increasing her self-esteem and building her emotional resilience is something you can do as well. I figured out why Leslie was second-guessing herself. She wanted to be perfect. If she couldn't be perfect, then she doubted she could do it at all. She let that go and decided to take the steps necessary to find peace within herself and her personal and professional relationships.

Learn to Let Go

Letting go is one of the most challenging tasks for human beings. When you are angry or holding a grudge against someone, the only person it affects is you. I had a client a few years back who realized she was still hurting from her parents' divorce when she was five years old. She felt abandoned by her dad. It was only after he died that she realized that her parents' divorce had everything to do with her father's issues and nothing to do with her.

Letting go isn't easy, but you can take baby steps in the healing process. In this chapter, I will explain how to express your frustrations, learn about forgiveness and living a self-aware life. Here's how:

WRITE A LETTER ABOUT YOUR FEELINGS

Getting words on paper about how you feel is a powerful therapeutic tool to sort out your thoughts about someone or an experience you've had. Writing a letter allows you to express yourself in ways that your emotions may make difficult to do verbally. Here's how:

1. Grab a sheet of paper or a piece of stationery and go somewhere you can be alone for 30 minutes.

2. Address the letter to the person or the painful experience.

3. Write the letter as if you are talking to the person or the experience.

4. Share your emotions about everything you remember from that experience or about how the person hurt you.

5. When you've signed the letter, reread it. Meditate or sit in silence for a few minutes.

6. Now, take that letter and burn it. Yes, burn it. I want you to let it go! (Always keep safety precautions in mind and burn it in a fireplace or firepit.)

The motivation behind writing this letter is to learn how to start forgiving. We'll talk more about forgiveness, but this is a great first start.

WRITE A LETTER TO YOUR PAST SELF

Have you done something you can't stop feeling guilty or bad about? It may have happened when you were a child or maybe it was just last week. Many of my clients beat themselves up for their past choices. I tell them, "Ladies, give yourself grace. It happened for a reason. Allow yourself to forgive yourself and let it go." The "Dear Me" letter is one way to do this.

Follow the steps in the previous exercise, but this time, write to your past self. If you can, pull out a picture of yourself at the age you were when you made a choice that makes you feel bad about today and keep it beside you as you write.

In this letter you are opening up to yourself, giving your permission to let it go and move on. Again, take time to reread it before you take step 6.

This is a freaking powerful exercise. I did this exercise for an experience I had in first grade. After I reread my letter and looked at the photo of my five-year-old self, I started crying, and all the negative feelings I felt about the incident washed away with my tears.

MAKE "I AM" STATEMENTS

"I Am" statements are often referred to as self-affirmations or positive self-talk. If it's not ahead of your time, you may remember the *Saturday Night Live* character Stuart Smalley telling his reflection in the mirror how much he loved himself. While that was just a silly skit, there's something to telling yourself that you love you. We all talk to ourselves, and what we say can be both positive and negative. Occasionally, you may find yourself saying things like, "I am not good enough. I am not pretty enough. I am not perfect enough," etc. Changing negative talk to positive talk is a powerful motivational strategy.

Changing your self-talk will change your external circumstances. Let's put together some "I Am" statements just for you! Think about all of your positive qualities as you do this exercise:

1. Grab your journal and go into a room with a mirror.

2. Stand in front of the mirror, look yourself in the eyes, and say, "I am *(fill in the blank)*." Write it down.

3. Look at yourself again and say, "I am *(fill in the blank)*." Write it down.

4. Keep this process going for about 15 minutes.

When you're done, you should have at least 30 "I Am" statements in your journal. Read them daily and commit a few to memory. Say them when you are brushing your teeth, cooking dinner, or about to hop into a meeting. That lady in that mirror is a powerful woman!

Release Your Cynicism

We all experience disappointment in life, and let's be honest, it freaking sucks. But holding on to those experiences and assuming that's the way it's always going to be won't pave the way to a more meaningful life. Admitting that you are cynical is the first step to releasing it. Limiting your time on news and social media can help you regain some of your hope and faith in the world and yourself. I suggest to my clients that they limit their consumption to 15 minutes in the morning and 15 minutes in the evening.

Most important, surround yourself with positive people. Have you heard American entrepreneur Jim Rohn's quote, "You're the average of the five people you spend the most time with"? That's pretty powerful insight. You can choose to hang with other cynics, or you can hang with people who put a positive spin on life and help you see the bright side. Having hope and faith in yourself and the outer world is an excellent way to maintain your motivation in all areas of yourself.

ACKNOWLEDGE THE GOOD PARTS

Do you look at the glass as half full or half empty? What would your life look like and where would it take you if you always considered your glass at least half full? When I think about this analogy, I think about how much spark and joy little kids have when they are playing. Their glass always seems to be half full.

We don't often take time to acknowledge when life was good. Instead, we tend to look at life when things were tough. Let's look now at the good parts. Pull out your journal and think back to a time when you felt happy and alive and you loved what you were doing. Respond to the following questions in your journal:

1. What were you doing?

2. How did you feel?

3. Why were you doing it?

4. Were you with anyone? If so, who?

5. How old were you when was this happening? 10 years old? 25 years old? 40 years old?

The key to acknowledging the good parts of your life is to intentionally remember those moments when you loved every part of your soul; this will help motivate you to find the spark and joy you once experienced.

AUDIT YOUR FRIENDSHIPS

The people you are friends with can impact how you view life. Who are you connecting with on social media? What are your Facebook groups like? Are you friends with people on social media who are Debbie Downers when it comes to political views or life? You *can* unfollow or unfriend them. It is okay! Who are the flesh-and-blood people you consider friends? You can unfriend or unfollow human beings who don't bring joy into your life, too!

Maybe you've had a friend since grade school, but they seem stuck in the past while you've made great strides in self-growth. What can you do in a case like that? Don't reach out as often and don't accept invitations to hang out with them as often. I understand that this is challenging, but keep your goals in mind. Make room for positive friendships that motivate you to live your best life.

Bet on Forgiveness

There has likely been a time in your life when you were hurt by a parent, friend, romantic partner, etc. Whomever it was, if you haven't resolved those feelings, now is a perfect time. The type of forgiveness I'm talking about isn't about finding them on the street, walking up to them and shouting, "I forgive you!" and then walking away. It's really about giving a gift to yourself—to feel better, to enjoy life, and to not be a Debbie Downer.

Try to see the situation from another perspective to potentially help you release unwanted feelings. Get out your journal and respond to the following:

- What was that person dealing with at the time? Were they under stress?

- Did something from their past possibly trigger their behavior? What might have happened to them?

- Was something going on in their life that may have caused their behavior?

- Did you do something to trigger them?

- If you could imagine them apologizing, what would they say?

- Write a letter of forgiveness to that person, with the understanding that this is for your eyes only.

FORGIVE OTHERS

When you forgive, you will experience a sense of relief in your life, and you will have a glow about you. People may even wonder what you are doing differently! Forgiveness is all about moving on. It's no longer dwelling on the person or situation that hurt you. It's about leaving the past behind and moving toward the future with purpose and motivation.

Grab your journal, take a couple of deep breaths, and respond to the following prompts:

1. Write down three to five names of people you haven't forgiven and why you haven't forgiven them.

2. Take a few more deep breaths and look at it from their perspective as you just learned to do, focusing on one person at a time.

3. Who is this person to you? How do you feel toward them? Do you still want them in your life?

4. Do you believe you are gaining something by not forgiving someone? Might your hurt and anger be hurting you more than it is hurting them, if it is at all?

5. Write a few more sentences addressed to that particular person, explaining what you were feeling and why. For example, "I value your friendship, Mary, but I was hurt when I came to you in confidence about my relationship issues with my spouse. I found out you talked about it with someone else. I am furious at you, but I forgive you. I want to discuss this with you so it will not happen again."

Keep in mind that this strategy is for *you,* not them. Remember, your goal is to stay motivated to make positive changes with regard to your emotional health rather than stay stuck in the past.

FORGIVE YOURSELF

Usually, when we think about forgiveness, we tend to think about the person who hurt us, but we can also forgive ourselves.

Do the previous exercise on a separate sheet of paper and name yourself this time. Spend a good 30 to 60 minutes on this one, writing as much as you can.

Once you finish the writing exercise, step away for a day or two, and then reread it. You can tuck it away in your journal or you may choose to burn it (safely). It's up to you. Either way, let it go!

Self-Sabotage Isn't Pretty

Self-sabotage is when you let your insecurities get the best of you, messing things up in your mind. It's your mind giving you a way out of a situation when you may feel there is simply too much at stake and you may not be able to take the outcome of failure or rejection. It's one of the best ways to crush your motivation, and we don't want that! When I think of self-sabotage in my life, I think of the outrageous mistakes I made in college (my head's shaking right now).

As you look back on your life, I want you to think about those times that you did self-sabotage. Now, I want you to stop putting yourself down about it. Learn more about how to do so in the next sections.

STOP PUTTING YOURSELF DOWN

We all have those days when we berate ourselves. "I am fat/skinny. I am not pretty/good enough. He/she would never want to be with me. They don't love me." And the list goes on and on. On days when you're feeling particularly terrible about yourself, listen to the stories you are making up. Where are they coming from? Why are they popping up in your head? What caused this mindset?

Recognize that you had that negative thought and then turn it around. For example, if you're thinking, "I am not pretty," bring to mind the qualities you do like about yourself and reframe: "There are things about my features that are attractive, such as my high cheekbones and smile."

Also, if someone gives you critical feedback that you agree with on some level, avoid getting down on yourself. Instead, look at the criticism as a gift that motivates you to do better. For example, if your boss criticizes your work, you may immediately fall back on negative thoughts such as "I am not good enough. I am not right for this job." Instead, recognize that you are getting feedback, which you can use to change. Feedback and criticism can be good motivators to improve.

FEAR OF . . .

Fear can be a huge obstacle to motivation. Fear of failure, for instance, can wreck your motivation to begin something new. Fear of the future can keep you stuck in the past. Fear of flying can keep you from going on an important business trip. The list can be never-ending.

While you may not get rid of the fear entirely, you can learn to lessen its impact. Here's a helpful mindfulness exercise you can use to work through your fears:

1. Go to a quiet place and get comfortable.

2. Ask yourself, "What am I most afraid of?"

3. Take a breath and then ask yourself, "Why am I afraid of this?" Is it the fear of failure, of the unknown, of abandonment, or something else? What was happening in your life the first time you remember feeling this fear?

4. Now ask yourself where you are holding this fear. Is it in your mind, your body, your heart? Take a few breaths to try to soften that spot.

5. What is happening right now that's causing this fear to surface? Remind yourself that it's okay to fear something and still move forward. That takes courage, and you have it.

Live a Self-Aware Life

When I think about living a self-aware life, it isn't a textbook version of the experience. It's about recognizing how I play a larger part in the universe and acknowledging the messages I receive for my next best steps. Let me give two real-life examples:

- A friend of mine sees cardinals whenever she needs guidance (cardinals represent her deceased grandmother). A cardinal prompts her to check in with herself.

- My client and I were chatting about her next steps for her business. She was frustrated with a project for a client that had reached a standstill. I said, "Let it go. Stop worrying about it. Throw it in the trash." She pretended to ball it up and throw it in the trash and then moved on to other things. Within six hours, she heard from the client with instructions to move forward.

How about you? Have you ever experienced a scenario similar to this: You rush out the door to head to work but realize you left your purse in the house and go back to retrieve it. Then, as you are driving to work, you see that a terrible accident occurred right around the time you would have been on the road. You look up and say, "Thank you!"

Things like this happen all the time. You can develop your awareness to notice them.

SELF-AWARENESS IS A MUSCLE—USE IT.

You build muscles in your body by exercising, and ideally, you do this daily. When you exercise your self-awareness muscle, as I want you to do on this journey, you're giving yourself an opportunity to adjust circumstances and receive guidance to live your best life.

Here are a couple of ways to build this muscle:

Recognize that it's okay to adjust your goals and dreams. The project you want to launch hasn't gotten off the ground because your manager is too busy to approve your proposal. Adjust your deadlines. You were being guided to not launch at this time.

Look for lessons, not excuses. If you fail at something or fall short of your expectations, figure out how you can improve rather than focusing on reasons (aka excuses for) why something didn't happen. Make your lessons count.

Prove yourself wrong. Think you can't do something? Think again. Have you ever wanted to accomplish a 5K; start your own company; or, heck, throw a Pinterest birthday party for your daughter? Prove to yourself that you can by doing it!

Working your self-awareness muscle takes practice. You have to show up every day! When you are self-aware, you'll know that it's okay to fail. It happened for a reason. You may not be able to figure it out right then and there, but that's okay! Just keep your eyes and mind open.

WATCH YOUR THOUGHTS, EMOTIONS, AND ACTIONS

Read this quote from Chinese philosopher Lao Tzu a couple of times, and then grab your journal: *Watch your thoughts, they become your words; watch your words, they become your actions; watch your actions, they become your habits; watch your habits, they become your character; watch your character, it becomes your destiny.* Spend some time responding to these questions to evaluate your starting point:

- What are the thoughts you think daily?

- What are the emotions you feel daily?

- What are the actions you take daily?

All three of these things are totally within your control. You can choose to be in a positive or negative mindset. You can choose to lift yourself up or put yourself down. You can choose to get out of bed and go for a walk or sleep in. What will you choose?

Find Self-Acceptance

There are days when you are crushing life, and there are days when nothing seems to be going right. It's par for the course. Something that's helped me through the highs and lows is finding self-acceptance. Like self-awareness, practicing self-acceptance is very much like exercising a muscle. Being accepting of whatever is going on in life can motivate you to move forward because you'll no longer be stuck on judging yourself.

BE KIND TO YOURSELF

When I transitioned to my coaching businesses, I was surprised to discover how hard many of my clients were on themselves. The negativity. We all do it, right? Learning to be kind to yourself is the best way to keep up your motivation.

Grab your phone and send yourself a text message that names three qualities about yourself that you admire. If you can't think of any (I hope you can!), ask a friend, partner, or family member to name three. Did you get the text? Did it make you feel good? Make sending kind texts to yourself a fun daily habit.

FIGURE OUT YOUR NON-NEGOTIABLES

It's Sunday night. You look at your calendar and freak out. You need to present your new marketing strategy at work on Friday and your partner is out of town. After school you have to chauffeur your kids to different activities. You are wondering how you are going to fit your workouts in. Now you feel pissed off because the week is starting off on the wrong foot—and it hasn't even started yet!

Let's clear that brain of yours every Sunday before you head into the week ahead. Pull out your day planner, and let's use this scenario as an example:

1. What are the non-negotiables? Fill them into your day planner:

    *   Workout and shower: 6:00 to 7:30 a.m.

    *   Work: 8:30 a.m. to 4 p.m.

    *   Dinner, homework, and kids in bed: 6:30 to 8:30 p.m.

    *   "Me" time: 8:30 to 10:30 p.m.

2. Figure out what you can do to make your day go more smoothly by taking care of what you can the night before:

    *   Get your work clothes and workout clothes ready.

    *   Make sure the kids have what they will need in the morning.

- Can you arrange for another parent to help with drop-offs and pickups? Can you tag team? Make any necessary phone calls.

3. At work, spend one hour in the morning and one hour in the afternoon working on your marketing strategy. Turn off ALL notifications and put your phone in your purse. After each hourly session, clear your head, go to lunch, or grab a coffee. Take care of the other work-related activities you need to and come back to it. That gives you eight hours in four days to finish your marketing scheme.

4. Grab something ready-made (but nutritious!) at the grocery store for dinner on your way home.

5. Spend time with the kids and get them into bed.

6. Enjoy your me time and relax knowing that you are going to present the best marketing strategy to your boss on Friday afternoon because you will review the final touches that morning!

I realize that this looks like a perfect setup, but I hope you can see that writing out your life like this versus keeping it in your head can keep you motivated to get everything you need to get done, done. There's no need to stress about it when you have a clear plan.

Live with Purpose

Life has to be more than get up, take kids to school (if you have them), go to work, make dinner, go to bed, and repeat. Right? Living with purpose reflects who you are deep inside. To help you sort out your purpose, grab your journal and respond to these five questions:

1. What is most important to you in your life? Family, faith, community, freedom, or something else?

2. What would you want someone to say at your eulogy? What do you want to be known for?

3. Do you volunteer at a nonprofit or help out your community? (That's the topic of chapter 9.)

4. Do you wake up and go to bed every night with gratitude? Do you thank the Universe or your higher power for another day?

5. Are you aligned with your career? Does your job fuel your soul?

One of my clients loves to volunteer her time, whether it's delivering food to the elderly or helping college students with their résumés. She finds purpose in helping others. Spend time thinking about your purpose; it doesn't have to be volunteering. Perhaps your purpose is to inspire others, facilitate connection between people, or live mindfully.

When you start living with purpose, life seems a bit more relaxed because you've figured out what makes you dance and your heart sing. Return to these questions if you lose your motivation to do something. Maybe your purpose has changed, and if so, that's okay. Adjust those sails; the Universe has got you!

IDENTIFY YOUR VALUES

It's essential to know what you value because these are the guiding principles of your life. According to *Oxford English Dictionary*, values are "a person's principles or standards of behavior; one's judgment of what is important in life." Core values are your driving factor.

If you aren't clear on your values, you may not recognize what motivates you. Grab your journal, and follow these steps to help you figure out what drives you:

1. Do an internet search for "examples of core values."

2. Review the list and choose 15 to 30 values that resonate with you and write them down.

3. Group similar values together into five groups.

4. Review each group and choose one value that resonates with you the most from each group.

5. Write the heading "My Core Values" and list your five top picks.

There are no wrong answers here! This is personal to you. Here's an example from one of my clients (the bolded ones were her five top picks from each category):

Freedom	Family	**Love**	Balance	Fun
Abundance	Loyalty	Kindness	**Health**	**Happiness**
Independence	**Caring**	Relationships	Well-Being	Playful

Knowing your core values is part of your repertoire of tools for keeping yourself motivated. If you feel stuck and can't move forward, head back to your core values to see if you can identify your driving factors for that situation to get you moving again.

PASSION IS ENERGY

Once you figure out your values, you can begin living with purpose, and living with purpose energizes you. The energy you put out there can be directed toward yourself, your family, your job, volunteering, a passion project, crafts and hobbies—whatever you are excited about. You will notice that you are alive for a reason and you're not just going through the motions, living yet another Groundhog Day.

Here are a few examples of how your purpose and values can energize you:

• Your purpose is to inspire others and you value fitness, so you start training to be a fitness instructor, even if your training sessions have to be at 5:00 a.m. before your family gets moving.

- Your purpose is to contribute to society and you value creative expression, so in the evenings, you focus on a creative side business with services that will benefit your community.

- Your purpose is to help others and you value service to others, so at lunchtime, you volunteer your time at a soup kitchen.

When you discover what fuels your soul, what makes you smile, and what makes you want to live your best life, you'll find ways (and time) to feel emotionally fulfilled. Why? Because you're motivated. Always keep in mind, though, that there will be days when you don't feel motivated and your self-confidence begins to wane. When that happens, go back to the basics (food, water, and sleep); honor your body if it needs fuel or rest. Don't expect to be 100 percent, 100 percent of the time!

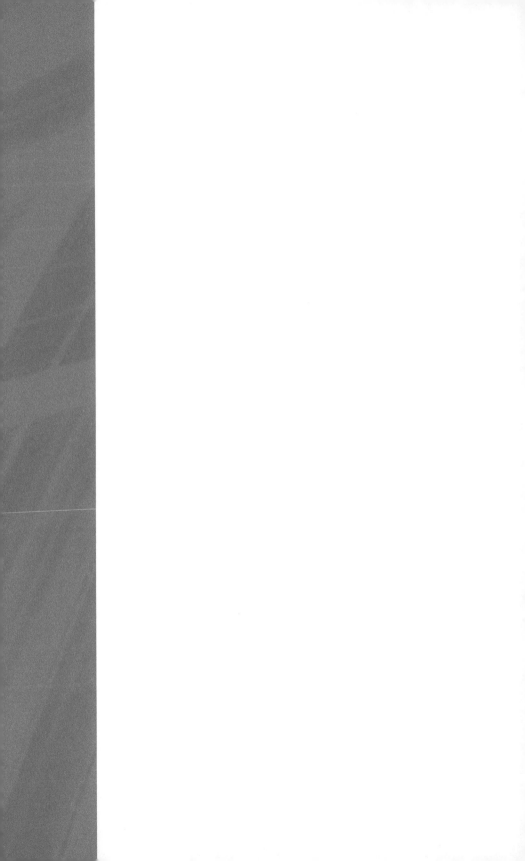

CHAPTER FIVE

There's No Such Thing as a Tribe of One

Personal Relationships

Personal relationships are the best, right? From the unconditional love of a parent to the touch of a lover to the belly laughs with friends and even business partnerships—all these things are possible because of other people. But let's be real, there can also be hurt, heartache, frustrations, and everything in between when others are involved. This chapter gives you a look at the good, the bad, and the ugly in relationships to help you assess where you currently are, where you want to be, and how to find the motivation to get there.

MEET JESSICA

I met Jessica when she signed up for my program "Monarch Mindset Coaching" to reset and focus on the positives in her life. She was the co-owner of a real estate company in Boerne, Texas. She wanted to make her business and her life more impactful. Her biggest obstacle was that she had difficulty communicating with her business partner. She mentioned that she'd often get frustrated in her other relationships as well.

We discussed her frustrations and how she was always looking for people to respond to her in the way she expected. I coached her to try to stop getting others to change by reversing the roles and figure out how *she* could change her relationships. I gave her an exercise that I learned when I worked at lululemon athletica, which I use regularly for myself and with my clients. It's called "Above or Below the Line."

Jessica divided a piece of paper in half so that there was a line running horizontally through the center.

I instructed her to write a few phrases about her qualities when she is "above the line" with regard to her relationships. She wrote: "I listen. I take time to respond thoughtfully. I ask questions. I do research. I pull my weight. I hold myself accountable. I am in control."

Then I instructed her to write a few phrases when she is "below the line." She wrote: "I blame others. I react harshly. I ignore them. I find fault in how they respond or react. I expect them to take care of things I want done. I have no control. It's everyone else's fault."

Jessica began using the "Above or Below the Line" concept in her interactions with others, always trying to stay *above* the line. She was motivated to make a change within herself for both her business and her personal life. Over the course of our sessions, I saw a shift in her mindset within weeks of doing this exercise, and she started making great strides in her business. Currently, Jessica and her business partner are thriving in Texas with a better relationship and guidance from each other.

Like Jessica, when you are "above the line," you are in your element. Nothing is going to stop you, and you are taking responsibility for your actions. When you are "below the line," you are not in the right place. You may play the blame game or make tons of excuses for why this is happening *to* you. In other words, you don't own up to your part in the relationship. (You'll have a chance to do this exercise soon!)

Use Your Words

One of the hardest parts of relationships is expressing yourself clearly and concisely, because it doesn't always come naturally. You have to be vulnerable, and that is seldom enjoyable. In Brené Brown's book *Daring Greatly,* she discusses vulnerability. She writes, "Daring greatly means the courage to be vulnerable. It means to show up and be seen. To ask for what you need. To talk about how you're feeling. To have the hard conversations."

Knowing that vulnerability is a quality you need to embrace, how can you improve your communication skills with your partner, family, or friends?

Let's dig a tad deeper into responding versus reacting and then let's look at how to use your words to motivate you to have better personal relationships. We are all works in progress, so give yourself grace if you don't get it right away.

RESPOND, DON'T REACT

Responding and reacting may look similar, but they *feel* different. Let's say you are having a conversation with your partner about your dinner plans, and they make a comment about what you're cooking *again*, and it triggers you. Suddenly, you feel unappreciated for your efforts. You react with a quip about them cooking for themselves if they don't like it. A response would be hearing what they've said and asking yourself, "What did they mean by that? It sounds like they don't like what I'm preparing." See the difference?

To start responding instead of reacting, keep the acronym PAVE in mind:

Pause: If you feel triggered, pause for a moment. If someone wants an answer right away, let them know you're thinking about it.

Action: Prepare to respond to what they said by reversing the roles and thinking about how you would want to feel.

Voice: Calm your voice before you speak, and voice your response with grace. (There's more on this following section.)

Evaluate: How did your interaction go? Was it successful? Did it help you and the other person communicate effectively?

Carry this acronym with you in your toolbox. This can be used not only for your personal relationships but during business conversations as well.

YOUR TONE WILL TELL

Whether you are talking calmly, raising your voice to speak about an issue, yelling, or saying nothing at all, your voice can play a significant role in all your conversations. Is there a right way to use your voice? Think about how you feel when someone raises their voice at you. It doesn't feel good, does it? Think about how you feel when someone mutters or speaks barely audibly. That doesn't feel good either. Think about when their voice is dripping with sarcasm. Enough said. There are so many ways to use our voices, and they have the power to elicit strong feelings in others.

When you are interacting with others, ask yourself these important questions:

1. Is your voice projecting more than it needs to?

2. Is your voice laced with negative emotions?

3. Is your voice being heard?

4. Are you not speaking up at all?

That last one can hurt more than not expressing your truth. Always use your voice to speak your truth and be authentic, but remember to PAVE the way. You'll thank yourself for it later.

Embrace Empathy

Empathy is the ability to share and understand the feelings of another person. To improve relationships, you need to learn how to step into someone else's shoes and understand their feelings and views. This isn't always easy. There are three types of empathy: cognitive, emotional, and compassionate. We'll discuss each of these soon.

For now, here are three techniques to motivate yourself to start being more empathetic and improve your relationships, including the one you have with yourself:

Ask yourself better questions: How can you be better toward yourself? How can you be your own cheerleader so that you can be a better example for others?

Get feedback: Ask for feedback from people you are close to regarding your listening and communication skills.

Explore your heart, not just your head: You can read or ask questions all day long, but you also need to feel in your heart for answers.

I'LL STAND BY YOU (COGNITIVE)

Cognitive empathy is seeing something from someone else's perspective. For example, the next time your girlfriend complains about her annoying boyfriend (again!), listen to what she's saying; it's one of the most productive things you can do. Rather than jump on her for complaining, empathize with her frustration and ask what she needs from you without judgment. A friend to listen to her? Advice? A shoulder to cry on? Try to share her frustration rather than get frustrated by her—and always keep what she tells you in confidence.

When you let your friends know you will stand by them, they will be open and vulnerable with you, and your connections will deepen.

LEAN ON ME (EMOTIONAL)

When I think of emotional empathy, I think of other people's feelings—like when someone is hurting, you feel the pain, too. A great example of this is the mother-child connection. If a mom stares at her baby and smiles, the baby smiles back. The opposite holds true, too. Ever been in a room with a group of toddlers? One kid starts crying, and before you know it, the others are crying, too.

Emotional empathy deepens relationships with friends, family members, and partners, especially when they are struggling or in distress. Funerals are a good example of this: When someone experiences a loss, you can feel their pain, even if you didn't know the person who passed all that well, if at all.

When I think of emotional empathy and connecting with others, I've learned a few lessons I'll share with you:

Talk to other people. There's no better way to build emotional empathy than to interact with others and ask them how they are feeling, even if you don't know them all that well. My mom loves to strike up conversations with strangers. She always asks how they are doing and listens for their response. It is the sweetest thing. I used to roll my eyes and be like, "Mommmmm," but now that I'm older, I realize I do the same thing!

Observe body cues. You can often tell how someone is feeling if you look at their body language. Slumped shoulders? Tears in their eyes? A smile on their face? This says a lot about how someone is feeling and gives you an opportunity to empathize.

Listen to them. Hear what they're saying. Let them express their highs and lows.

Take action. There was a grumpy man I used to see all the time. I'd acknowledge his grumpiness with a little frown and then I'd say, "Good morning," to him with a smile. Soon enough, he started greeting me with a smile of his own. (You can make a difference in someone else's day. Do it!)

BE THERE (COMPASSIONATE)

When I think about the importance of compassionate empathy, which is what motivates someone to help, I'm reminded of when I had two miscarriages in a row and my dad's passing. Some of my friends would call to see how I was doing, which I always appreciated, but other friends would call and say, "We want to take you out for dinner and drinks tonight" or "Pack a bag, we're going to the beach." Those friends helped me grow as a human being because they supported me through some of the most challenging times of my life.

Sometimes, you need to take action to help a friend or a family member out. And this is what compassionate empathy is all about. Here are some ideas for helping someone in a time of need:

Be specific with your offer. Sometimes statements like, "Let me know what you need," or "I am praying for you," are too vague. To express compassionate empathy, you could say something like, "I am heading to the grocery store, what can I get for you?" Or "Can I come over to help you organize the stuff in your dad's closet?"

Only offer help you can genuinely provide. You may not want to offer to take them to a therapy session if it's in the middle of your workday, but you might want to offer to pay for a taxi to get them there. If you say you are coming over during the weekend to help them organize but then your schedule gets too busy, not following through will be hurtful. So offer only what you can actually do.

A small gesture goes a long way. If you can't arrange time to devote to your friend in need, a small gesture can mean a lot to them. A quick text message or a funny meme may brighten their day. You can also send an old-fashioned Hallmark card or a write quick letter and send it in the mail.

Make the First Move

Sometimes, if a relationship is on shaky ground, it will be up to you to make the first move. For example, maybe you don't have the best relationship with one of your parents, but you need to share something that has been bothering you. Or you and your partner have been on the outs and you need to have a tough conversation. Perhaps you have a teen you want to connect with better.

Having those hard conversations—whether they are with a parent, a sibling, a coworker, kids, a friend, or a partner—can make a lot of people nervous. I've seen it with many of my coaching clients. Why? Many people envision the worst possible outcome. The next few strategies can help motivate you to start those hard conversations, as challenging as they might be, and work toward a positive outcome. Remember to be authentic and talk from your heart.

GET CLARITY

Before you start a serious conversation, get clear on what you want to say. If you're going to be motivated to have a reliable and successful chat, using the right words will be the key to your success. Here's some advice that I share with my clients to get them ready to have a tough conversation:

1. Take some time by yourself. Step away from devices, kids, work, or anything else that might distract you. Don't use headphones or listen to music. As much as possible, let the sounds of nature be your music.

2. Set a timer for at least 20 minutes.

3. Take a few deep, relaxing breaths, and think about the ideal conversation you want to have. What will you say? How will you say it? What will they say in response? What are you feeling?

4. Visualize the conversation going perfectly.

5. When the timer goes off, take another deep breath, and then move on to the next strategy.

WRITE OUT YOUR FEELINGS

Once you've visualized your conversation and felt all the feels, pull out your journal. Respond to these who, what, when, where, and why questions:

- Who are you talking to? Parent, partner, child, boss?

- What is the topic all about? A childhood memory, finances, an issue at work?

- When are you going to talk to them about it? Over the weekend, during the week, first thing in the morning?

- Where will you have this conversation? Will it be a neutral ground? At home, outdoors, a conference room?

- Why is this conversation important to you? Why do you feel the need to open up about this issue? Were you hurt by what someone said or did?

While I realize that this exercise seems robotic, your conversation will flow more naturally because you'll have a clear idea of what you want to say and how. Keep your notes with you if that helps you be clear.

Set Firm Boundaries

Setting firm boundaries in your relationships can be tricky, especially if you are a people pleaser, but they are essential for healthy relationships. If someone oversteps your boundaries, it can leave you feeling unappreciated or taken advantage of. If they don't know what your boundaries are, this is more likely to happen.

Knowing where you stand is essential, and so is starting small if you aren't comfortable with the idea of setting boundaries. Some strategies for both are up next.

MAKE A STAND

Do you use your voice to say what is on your mind? If not, you may need to take a stand. My client Marybelle went back to graduate school and found herself dealing with a harsh professor. She left their conversations feeling distraught, stressed, and in tears. Her work was suffering and she needed to set some boundaries with that professor. The next time she met with him and was berated for the poor quality of her work, Marybelle told him that she was looking for constructive feedback, not demoralizing comments.

Do you need to take a stand on something? Here's how to go about it:

1. Educate yourself on the topic or your position. Have supporting data if you might need it.

2. Is the person you are discussing the issue with willing to listen to your point of view? If not, consider whether it's worth the frustration.

3. Respect the other person's opinion; you may have to agree to disagree, unless you are requesting that another person respect your boundaries.

START SMALL

Taking small steps is one of the best ways to build simple habits to stay motivated when setting boundaries with others. Start by knowing what you will and won't tolerate in your relationships. Unclear on that? Take these steps:

1. Build your self-esteem and self-confidence. Taking control of what you can (your health and wellness, learning to let go, and living a self-aware life) will help you start recognizing what mutual respect looks like in a relationship.

2. Notice your emotional, physical, and mental state in response to someone's actions toward you. For example, if a coworker asks a personal question about your relationship with your partner, notice how their question makes you feel. Uncomfortable? Say so. You know your boundaries in your gut and heart.

3. Practice setting boundaries. For instance, tell that coworker you'd prefer not to discuss your relationship because it's personal. That's boundary-setting. Keep practicing!

You Have Time

Relationship-building takes time. You can't rush into a deep relationship on day one, or even month one, and maybe not even year one. However, many people want to rush headlong into a new romantic relationship because it feels so good, and they want a commitment right away in an effort to control the future. It happens with new friendships, too. That's the fear of the unknown at play. You'd rather know the outcome now versus allowing time for the relationship to grow and develop.

When you find yourself stressing over how a relationship will turn out: 1) Pause and say, "This relationship is exactly where it needs to be" and 2) Head outside, look up at the sky, and say, "Thank you for the opportunity to explore this relationship."

Even if you aren't heading into a new romantic relationship, the next three motivational strategies can help you take the time you have (and need) to put your best self forward in any new relationship.

FIND YOURSELF FIRST

You have to know who you are before you bring someone new into your life. I'm reminded of the movie *Runaway Bride*. Julia Roberts's character would change herself for whichever relationship she was in. She claimed to like her eggs the way her fiancé at the time liked them. Fortunately, by the end of the movie, she figures out how she likes her eggs.

Do you know how you like your "eggs"? To figure out who you are (aka "find yourself"), grab your journal and respond to these prompts:

- You have one life! What fuels your soul?

- If money was no object, where would you live and what would you do?

- What types of people would you attract into your life?

- If you don't already have one, describe your ideal lover.

- If you are in a romantic relationship, describe how you each show up every day for each other.

- What is your favorite music to listen to? Why?

- What is your favorite movie? Why?

- What is your favorite book? Why?

- What are some of your other favorite things? Describe them.

- How do *you* like your eggs?

CHECK YOUR EGO

When I coached CrossFit, I would tell people to leave their ego at the door. Why? Because I didn't want them to hurt themselves by taking on too much weight or trying to "crush it" to prove themselves to others. The same goes for relationships. You don't want to take on so much that you end up crumbling or going over-the-top to try to prove that you're the best.

Here are some ways to keep your ego in check with regard to relationships:

1. Surrender the need to control things. You don't need to know how everything will work out. Just let it take its course.

2. Practice forgiveness. In other words, don't hold grudges; they can harm your relationships.

3. Reflect on your relationships with gratitude for what they add to your life.

4. Admit when you are wrong. Although this can be one of the hardest things to do, don't be afraid to say, "I messed up. I am sorry."

5. Respect others, as well as yourself.

FREE YOUR MIND

In the beginning of this chapter, I talked about the exercise I used with my client Jessica: "Above and Below the Line." Now it's your turn. This is an exercise in freeing your mind, because when you know when you are at your best and your worst, you have the freedom to choose.

Get a piece of paper and fold it in half horizontally or make a horizontal line in the middle of a fresh journal page. Bring to mind any relationship you want to look at and consider when you and the other person are operating above the line and when you are operating below the line.

Remember, when you are above the line, you are in your element and nothing can stop you, and when you are below the line, you are not in a good place, and one or both of you are not owning up to things.

1. Write all the best qualities of your relationship above the line and describe how you each act and respond when you are at your best. How do you feel when you are above the line?

2. Write out all the worst qualities of your relationship below the line and describe how you each act and respond when you are at your worst. How do you feel when you are below the line?

3. Now take a photo of it. Keep it somewhere you can look at it.

Doing this exercise can help you better recognize when you are below the line. Since it's not a great place to be, you'll be motivated to get back to the top!

Communication Is a Two-Way Street

Active listening plays a huge role in all relationships but there's more to having a good conversation. Being a good listener isn't simply being quiet or murmuring "mmm-hmmm" or repeating what the other person has said word for word. It's more about listening with your full attention, and then asking questions to learn even more. When both people in a conversation do this, it becomes a cooperative, enriching two-way dialogue.

Are you having dialogues like this with the people in your life? Are your conversations a one-way street or a two-way street? Are you truly communicating as best as you can with each other? Let's look at a couple of strategies to motivate you to have more enriching interactions and conversations with the people you care about.

MORE THAN WORDS

One of my favorite books is *The Five Love Languages* by Gary Chapman. Different people have different ways of expressing their love and different ways they prefer to receive love. The five love languages are: words of affirmation, acts of service, receiving gifts, quality time, and physical touch. Here are a few brief examples of each:

- Words of affirmation: "You did a great job!" or "You are beautiful."

- Acts of service: washing the dishes, taking care of the car's oil change

- Receiving gifts: a beautiful bouquet, tickets to a concert

- Quality time: going hiking, watching a movie

- Physical touch: caresses, kisses

How can you make the love languages work for you? I'll use a romantic relationship as an example, but even platonic friends may express their love most often in one of these five ways.

Here's how (take notes in your journal):

- Establish what your significant love language is. For example, do you express yourself physically, giving pats on the back, a kiss on the forehead, a caress? Or are you more verbal: "I love you so much!" I bet you have a good idea of your love language, but if you are unsure, you can take the quiz at 5LoveLanguages.com/quizzes/.

- Figure out what your partner's significant love language is. Does your partner shower you with affection, give you gifts every once in a while to show they appreciate you, spend uninterrupted time with you, etc.?

- Do your love languages work for each other? Neither of you are mind readers, so you need to tell each other what you want. Maybe your partner wants more quality time, or maybe you want them to do acts of service around the house. It's time to compromise. Remember, relationships are give-and-take. If your partner does an act of service, like taking care of the dinner dishes, you can give them quality time by putting your phone away and going for a walk together.

HAVE AN ENRICHING CONVERSATION

Let's combine active listening and being a good listener so that you can set yourself up to have an enriching two-way conversation. Try this the very next time someone engages you in conversation, and then practice it often:

1. Put your phone away.

2. Face the person and maintain normal eye contact.

3. Actively listen to what they are saying. Stay present. This helps you build trust and establish rapport.

4. Ask questions but don't bombard them with questions. Ask, listen, and respond.

5. Engage in the discussion, allowing it to be a two-way conversation.

I'll tell you as I tell my clients: Be the best listener you can be and show up in every conversation. I have a good friend in a mastermind group who is exceptionally present during our conversations. If he notices that one of us in the group is looking away or not paying attention, he'll call us on our BS, and I always appreciate the reminder.

Stay Present

This is one of my most challenging tasks. There is so much noise going on these days—work, errands, social media, the news, me time, family time—and, hey, what's for dinner? How do you stay present in a relationship with all that noise? First, you need to learn to be present for yourself.

Here's a straightforward tactic that I use with my clients and myself, especially during crazy, stressed-out times: For the first 15 minutes of every morning, don't do a dang thing. Sure, do your normal stuff (brush teeth, make coffee, go to the bathroom), but then go sit on the couch, your bed, the patio, or wherever. Just don't grab your phone or check your email. Instead, check in with yourself:

1. Where are you? What do you see? Birds, your partner getting dressed, the dog chasing his tail . . . ?

2. What do you hear? The airplane overhead, the neighbor's car starting, bird sounds . . . ?

3. What do you smell? The coffee in your cup, your partner's cologne or perfume, car exhaust . . . ?

4. What are you touching? Your warm coffee mug, the chair you're sitting in . . . ?

5. What are you tasting? That yummy coffee, your salty lips from your partner's early morning kiss . . . ?

THINK LIKE A TURTLE

In December 2019, I took a trip to Costa Rica. As I mentioned earlier, after my last Ironman Triathlon, I lost a little bit of myself. I just wanted to sit on a beach with no Wi-Fi, learn how to surf, run and cry whenever I wanted, *and* see baby turtles hatch and start their journey.

Those baby turtles would someday travel over 10,000 miles to return home as adults to lay their eggs. I watched them head into the water. Though they had *no* idea what would happen, they were determined to make it happen! They would have to deal with sharks, hurricanes, and birds waiting to snatch them up, but those little guys were motivated to get where they were going!

As we close this chapter, let the sea turtle's journey (which I saw on Pinterest and loved) motivate you to set out on your journey with confidence:

1. Life begins on the beach.

2. Sometimes you dig yourself out of a hole you didn't dig.

3. Keep the faith. You'll make it.

4. Never forget where you came from.

5. Life is better with a good friend.

CHAPTER SIX

Get Your Frida Kahlo On

Creativity

Has anyone ever asked you to draw or paint something? Did it make you laugh at the absurdity, cause you anxiety, excite you, or perhaps something else? What about writing or dancing? This is my jam, but maybe the idea of doing one or both gives you a hot flash! When I talk about creativity, I'm not talking about being the best artist, the smoothest dancer, or most creative marketing strategist. Creativity is about expressing yourself in whatever way works best for you. If you're not sure what that is but want to find the motivation to get your creative juices flowing, it's time to get your inner Frida on.

MEET STEPHANIE

I kept running into Stephanie in the locker room at my gym. She worked there, and she had this cool vibe going and beautiful brown flowing hair and tattoos covering nearly every part of her body. One day, she commented on my swimsuit, and then out of nowhere, asked, "Are you okay?" I wasn't exactly advertising it, but I told her I'd just lost my cat following a move and I didn't think it had ended well for him.

After we introduced ourselves, she said, "I don't think he is in this world anymore, but remember, he will always be with you." When I asked, "How do you know?" she told me she'd received a gift a while back and had started tapping into *that* world.

Our random chance meetings soon evolved into coffee talks and Zoom chats. When she lost her job at Life Time Fitness due to the COVID-19 lockdown, she said she wanted to start my coaching program. She'd felt that developing a relationship with me just before the pandemic was a message from the Universe to start her alternative and holistic health business. Stephanie lived her creativity, which was so different from other people's, that I knew she was gifted beyond what she knew. We sat down weekly and figured out what she needed to knock out to start her new business adventure by focusing on what she was good at.

Stephanie has a creative eye in her business. She gives excellent clairvoyant readings, which is a different type of creativity than some of us may be used to. Everyone has a different kind of invention. As we worked together, her creative juices began really flowing, and she came up with ideas like women's weekend retreats, yoga classes, and beautiful Energy Wreaths and manifesting kits. Her Energy Wreaths are made with love and different flowers, crystals, and shapes to help clear negativity from a space. Her manifesting kits combine tealights, herbs, flowers, and oils to bring forth energies one may need to manifest their journey. What I love about those is that they can serve as an extra push someone might need.

Stephanie and I also chatted about the basics of starting a business by figuring out who she was trying to serve, her ideal client, along with her mission statement and what services she was planning on offering. I had the opportunity to watch her blossom into a fantastic business owner. Using her creative skills, she stayed motivated to get her business up and running even during a lockdown. Her mindset switched because she was *forced* to change (extrinsic motivation, remember?) and start living her passion and hone in on her gifts as a spiritual teacher (intrinsic motivation). While Stephanie's creativity is different from singing, dancing, or drawing, her creative skills are reliable, and they work for her. I bet your creativity, whatever form it takes, will work for you, too.

Dream a Little

One of the most challenging aspects of wanting to achieve a goal so badly is being willing to let it go. What? When I wanted to qualify for the Ironman World Championship in Kona, Hawaii, it consumed me. I focused on that race so much that I didn't concentrate on the qualifying race I was doing that year. Realizing that I was doing this, I let the idea of qualifying go and focused on the task at hand.

What does this have to do with creativity? Stop *trying* so hard to be creative and allow yourself to simply focus on expressing your creativity in the moment. It doesn't matter what or how you create, just that you are giving yourself a chance to dream outside your usual box.

Let's look at a few strategies now to keep you motivated on your goal to expressing yourself in some creative way.

TO DRAW OR NOT TO DRAW

Have you heard that right-brain thinkers are the creative ones and left-brain thinkers are the ones who are strong at math and logic? (Insert eye roll.) As research continues on the brain, science is recognizing that it isn't so divided. Both sides of your brain need to work for you to fully function in this world. So, if you've always thought of yourself as uncreative, it's time to grab your journal, stop asking if you are creative or not, because you are! Think beyond the arts and literature:

1. Do you love building with LEGOs? What about gardening? Cooking? Creating strategic plans? Decorating? Doing your makeup? Hosting parties? Make a list of all the things you love to do. That's creativity!

2. How can you fit creativity into your life? Look at your list and see ways you can use your creativity. Love doing makeup? Offer to do a friend's. Love cooking? Make up your own recipe.

What you create doesn't have to be a huge painting you hang on your wall. And you don't have to build a ten-by-ten garden in your yard. How about just bringing a plant into your house, putting it in an attractive pot, and nurturing it?

PULL OUT YOUR INNER CHILD

Kids ask so many questions from "Why is the sky blue?" to "Why do people kiss?" They are innocent and are curious about everything—they also are very creative. Let's tap into your inner child and consider some questions you probably haven't been asked in a long while. Grab your journal, and respond to:

- If you could be a superhero, who would it be and why?

- What sounds do you like?

- Where is your favorite place to be?

- If you could be any animal, what would you be and why?

- If you could grow anything, what would you grow?

- What's a perfect day?

- Who makes you laugh? Why?

- If you could do anything right now, what would it be? (I would dance with my dad in heaven!)

Did you get your creative juices going? I bet you started thinking like a little kid again. Good for you. It's time to live!

STOP JUDGING YOURSELF

Mother Teresa said, "If you judge people, you have no time to love them." I'm going to change up that quote a little and say, "If you judge yourself, you have no time to love you." Why are we our own worst critics? Negative self-judgment can become an automatic habit, especially when it comes to expressing ourselves creatively. If you're judging yourself for not being creative enough or good enough at creativity, your creative mindset needs adjustment.

Grab your journal and start asking yourself these self-empowering questions:

1. What can I do to be more creative? For example, "I revisit what I enjoyed doing when I was young."

2. How can I find peace around the fact that I "can't" draw (or be creative in some other way you admire)? For example, "I sure can rock cutting pictures out of a magazine and making a vision board!"

3. What can I do differently to get a better outcome in my creativity? For example, "I can take classes on the type of art or other creative endeavor that interests me."

I want you to step away from judging yourself in *all* areas in your life, not just this one. I know it's challenging, but I promise you that those creative juices will start flowing if you stop criticizing yourself and start opening your mind to your potential.

Seek Out Inspiration

All artists seek out outside influences to help them create. Whether it is a walk in the park, research online, or reading a book, artistic influence is everywhere. Pablo Picasso's inspiration came from his lovers and objects such as African masks.

While you may not be a Picasso, here are three ways to find inspiration on your creative path:

1. **Change your environment.** Even during the lockdown of 2020. If I were writing and needed to change my setting, I would go outside to type and be inspired by the dragonflies and butterflies. Pre-2020, I would head to the coffee shop, put in my earbuds, and start writing.

2. **Watch a great film.** Whether it is *The Shawshank Redemption*, *Casablanca,* or *Black Panther,* great movies can inspire you to think differently, which is creativity in action.

3. **Watch an inspiring TED Talk.** Here are my top-three picks:

    *   Brené Brown's "The Power of Vulnerability"

    *   Simon Sinek's "How Great Leaders Inspire Action"

    *   Amy Cuddy's "Your Body Language May Shape Who You Are"

Remember your commitment to yourself to be more creative? Good. Keep looking for inspiration and go back to the places you find it. I watch these TED Talks at least once a quarter, because sometimes I need a little reminder.

INSPIRATION IS EVERYWHERE—EVEN IN THE GROCERY STORE

I love road trips and stopping at random gas stations. I generally go down the candy aisle and look for different types of bubble gum. When I get in the car, I time myself to see how long the flavor lasts and how big I can make the giant bubble. I pull out my creative side with bubble gum, and it's fun!

Here are a couple of ways to help you find your "bubble gum creativity" in your local grocery store:

1. Head to the candy aisle. Look at the names of the candies along with the branding and the logo. What caught your eye? What resonated with you? Did you like the lettering on one package but liked the logo on another?

2. Head to the cereal aisle. Ask yourself the same questions. The soda aisle? The snacks aisle? Do it all over again.

3. Now head to the produce department. Look at the shapes and sizes of the various fruits and veggies. Which shapes and colors are you drawn to?

A variation of this strategy that doesn't require you to step outside your home is to jump on social media and type in #art, #photography, or #costarica or whatever place inspires you. What do you see? Animals? Ocean? Sunset? Beach? Mountains? What do the images and colors mean to you? Inspiration *is* all around you. You just need to open your eyes and *feel*.

WHEN IN DOUBT, GO TO THE LIBRARY

When I went to Scotland with my mom, we decided to head into Edinburgh. We walked around town, and I found the coffee shop where J. K. Rowling wrote the Harry Potter series, The Elephant House. As we sat there I thought, "She had no idea that what she was writing at the time was going to become a best-selling brand."

The inspiration inside books is out of this world. Here are some of my favorite books, which I read for inspiration, and I encourage you to read them, too:

•   The Harry Potter series. Get into the creative mind of a best-selling author.

•   *The Alchemist* by Paulo Coelho. You can find your soul in this book.

- *The Four Agreements* by Don Miguel Ruiz. This one helps you find your freedom.

- *Daring Greatly* by Brené Brown. Learn how to be vulnerable.

If I need some motivation to get creative, I look at my photo in front of The Elephant House or dive into a good book with *no* phone and dream. Find books that inspire your creativity. You can even choose some books *on* creativity to get your creative juices flowing.

Take Lessons

Did you know that over five billion videos are watched every single day on YouTube? YouTube is so much more than music. Type in "how to draw/paint/dance/sing." It's there! Sweet. You can also sign up for live or virtual classes.

Schedule time each week to focus on a creative outlet that you're interested in. This will motivate you to keep your appointments. Your lessons can be virtual or in person. It's up to you. Let's look at both.

GO ONLINE

One of the things I want to learn is a foreign language. I took Spanish and French in high school, but I never learned enough to have a conversation. I started looking into Spanish classes online, and the opportunities were endless. I ended up grabbing one of the many apps available and started using it. I put a calendar reminder on my phone and on the app to remind me to practice for 15 minutes a day. That's it.

It's your turn. Whatever creative outlet interests you, type it into your internet browser or check out the apps for your smartphone. Do it now. Find a virtual class and commit to it.

LIVE LESSONS

While there are many opportunities online, sometimes I want to "head back to school" and get out of the house. Sticking to a schedule and set time is a motivational strategy in itself. You've made a commitment to someone to learn what they are teaching! Plus, when I am paying for a service or a class, it's an excellent motivator to get my booty in gear because I have skin in the game.

If you want to dive into your community to pull out your creative side, there are so many opportunities you just might enjoy. Here are a few resources that can help guide you and find what you need:

- Community colleges

- Libraries

- Meetup websites

- Local art clubs, like a photography group

- Eventbrite events

Find a Muse

A muse is a source of inspiration, often a person. Many artists have muses and rely on someone to help them shape their craft. Think about someone in your life who inspires or has inspired you to be creative? A child maybe? Have you ever gotten down on the floor with a little kid and helped them color a picture? Did you have a teacher who inspired you to do a bang-up science project? Yes, that took creativity.

To figure out who inspires you to be creative, think about your life from age one until now, breaking it up into however many decades you've lived. Get your journal; you're going to need it.

Here's how this might look for someone who's 30:

AGES	WHO INSPIRED ME?
1 to 10	Dad, older sister, best friend, art teacher
10 to 20	Boyfriend, best friend, English teacher
20 to 30	Professor, boss, musician, business owner

WHO INSPIRES YOU?

If you *need* to write, find a writer who inspires you. If you *need* to paint, find a painter who inspires you. This is real talk here. If you want to learn about love and crave a lover, find someone who inspires you to love. Now, look back at your list of muses, and answer the following questions:

1. How did each of those people help you express yourself?

2. Was it their looks? Their talent? How they made you feel? Their energy?

3. Is there a common theme among all your muses?

4. Can you look to one or more of them now to get inspired?

OH, THE PLACES YOU WILL GO

A place can also serve as your muse. For example, when I need to feel inspired, I think about the blue ocean or the sounds I heard when I was in Paris, France, or the sounds of nature when I walk in the mountains or forest. What places inspire you? What is your traveling muse?

- Big city or small town?

- A beach or mountains?

- Fancy hotel? Cabin? Condo? Airbnb?

- Cruise or camping?

- Lake or ocean?

- What inspires you about these places?

There is so much inspiration when it comes to looking beyond people; this world is beautiful. When I need to find my creativity, I head to Pinterest and type in "beaches," "Paris," or "Costa Rica," and my mind gets fueled with inspiration!

LOOK BEYOND A FACE OR A PLACE

A muse doesn't have to be a person or a place. It can also be an object or an animal. What inspires you when you see it? Swans? Rainbows? Flowers? Rocks? Geometric patterns? Any one of these things can be your object muse. When I see a robin, I'm reminded of my grandma, who loved them because she knew they were a sign of spring. My mom would call her every spring when she saw her first robin. Now, I do that with my mom. A robin inspires me to start fresh.

To find something that inspires you, ask yourself:

- What shapes are you attracted to? Circles, squares, triangles, octagons, etc.?

- What animals are you attracted to? Squirrels, monkeys, dolphins, whales, etc.?

- What insects are you attracted to? Butterflies, dragonflies, etc.?

- What birds are you attracted to? Eagles, hawks, cardinals, blue jays, etc.?

- What about a planet, or the sun, or the moon?

Can you combine a couple of these? Maybe circles attract you, reminding you of the sun. When you get 15 minutes of sunshine, you feel recharged to do your creative work!

Kill Perfection

I am a recovering perfectionist. Can you relate? Do you have the mindset that everything needs to be perfect? Newsflash: It does not. Whatever you are trying to do—write, dance, sing, paint, make wreaths, or whatever—"Just Do It." Thank you, Nike. If you want to get good at writing, you write. If you want to get good at dancing, you dance. If you want to get good at singing, you sing. I needed to get good at running, so I ran.

If you keep trying, will you become perfect at it? No. Again, there's no such thing. If you keep trying, you will build your skill, gain confidence, and start to grow; you just need to eliminate the idea that getting there will be perfect. The next strategy will motivate you to let that idea go!

PERFECTION IS FOR LOSERS

Why do some of us have the mindset that we must be perfect? For me, I thought I wasn't good enough. I didn't want to fail at my creative pursuits, which included starting a new business. I had the fear that if I didn't work hard enough, my business would fail. But once I let the idea of perfection go, I became a much better business owner.

So, how do you let go of the idea of being perfect? This is a tough one, but here are two simple strategies:

Build self-reliance. I have gone through some shit storms, but those storms brought me to where I am today. I am stronger and wiser, and know I have the resources and skills to do what I set my mind to do. Learn from your own challenges, and know that even though you're not perfect, you will survive.

Make your own decisions. I was once designing a triathlon racing kit, and I got so many opinions that I became overwhelmed and started second-guessing everything. My suggestion is to make your own decisions. Want to paint the room blue? Pick your own shade and paint it. Don't ask everyone to weigh in. Is it the perfect blue for everyone? No.

WHAT'S IN YOUR WAY?

When I feel a drive toward perfectionism and self-limiting beliefs creeping up and hindering my ability to be creative, I grab my journal, put on my headphones, and play my favorite classical music or a meditation piece. Then, I sit on the back patio as the sun is coming up and I ask myself three questions. Grab your journal; I want you to do this, too:

- What is holding you back from starting a creative project or activity?

- Why do you doubt yourself?

- What will happen if you fail?

On the top of a new page in your journal, jot down what you are trying to accomplish (for me, I might write something like: "Finish the blog," "Start the social media video," *or* "Complete Chapter Seven"). Now, ask yourself each question and write about it.

If I discover that what's blocking me is a fear of failure, I jot down my favorite quote: "What if I fail? Oh, my darling, but what if you fly?" Remember the quotes you were prompted to write in your journal on page 12? Revisit them and choose one now.

ADJUST YOUR STANDARDS

There are a couple of ways to adjust your standards—you can raise them, or you can lower them. The problem is, if you raise them too high, you might feel stressed out and as if you're half-assing everything. If you lower them, you may have no drive to get creative and get things done. What are realistic standards? Here's how to figure that out:

Gain clarity. What are you trying to accomplish? What is your goal with this project? What new behaviors do you have to learn?

Get real. What are your standards for this project? What do you want to accomplish? How do you want it to look when it's done? Are your current standards holding you back? Are they not challenging enough?

SLOW THE F DOWN

Are you speeding through life? Are you going from one appointment to the next with only five minutes to spare? Are you loading up on your meetings? Are you driving one child across town just to turn around and grab the other kid? We've been programmed to move and to think that if we don't keep moving, it means we're lazy. No wonder some of us have lost our creativity—there's no time to let the juices flow, let alone think.

Here are some strategies to slow down so that you can find the motivation to turn to your creative projects:

1. Cut back on things to do. I know this can be hard, but you do not have to be busy to enjoy life. Sometimes saying "no" is saying "yes" to yourself. It's okay to sit and enjoy life.

2. Go phone-free for one hour! Spend that hour gathering inspiration.

3. Find help. Yes, some of your tasks can be done by others. You don't have to do everything yourself!

4. Set aside time to do absolutely nothing. Even if that's just 15 minutes in the morning (see page 92).

LEARN TO BREATHE

My friend Mary Stockton, MA (MarysBreathJourneys.com) is a breathing-technique specialist. She says that proper breathing techniques can be used for stress release and even creativity. As a breath specialist, she's helped actors, dancers, graphic artists, and CEOs unlock and focus their mind on their talents. According to Mary, when you breathe from the nipple up, you are activating your sympathetic system (the "fight or flight" part of the nervous system), but when you breathe from your diaphragm, you are using your parasympathetic system (the "rest and digest" part). Obviously, we want to breathe from our diaphragms.

Here are two breathing techniques Mary taught me to start breathing from the diaphragm that you can try now:

- Lie on the floor. Place a book on your belly. Make the book rise as you breathe 5 to 10 times. When the book is rising, you are breathing from your diaphragm. Good job!

- Sit crisscross-applesauce style. Place a finger on your belly. Again, breathe 5 to 10 times, so that your finger moves with the expansion of your belly.

Proper breathing has a huge role in this journey of yours. Keep it in your back pocket and practice it daily.

So, did you finish your creative project? Good for you. I knew you had it in you. If you still haven't found your creativity, go back and revisit some of the exercises. You might not have identified your specific brand of creativity yet. There's always time to find it.

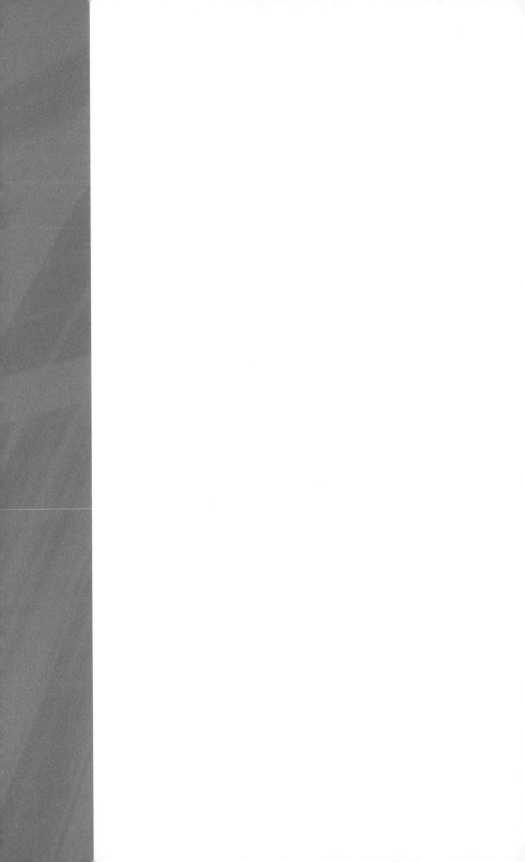

CHAPTER SEVEN

What Would Your Most Successful Friend Do?

Career and Wealth

Do you have a friend who is thriving in a fulfilling career and enjoying an abundance of success and personal wealth (it's not just about money)? What's her secret sauce? My guess is that she knows what she wants and is motivated to go for it. When it comes to your work life, do you feel excited or do you feel uninspired? The first step is getting clear on where you want to be so that you can be motivated to make change happen. Use the motivation strategies in this chapter to help you go places in your career and satisfy your need for personal and financial worth.

MEET JORDAN

Jordan, a fitness and nutrition coach, joined my program to help jump-start her nutrition business. She felt nervous about taking the business-owning plunge and was overthinking every step. Jordan needed to solidify her vision with a concrete plan and let go of her fear of the unknown and failure. As part of her initial interview, I asked her a number of questions, including, "What do you want to accomplish?" and "What is your limiting factor?" and "How do you take time for yourself? Workouts? Journaling? Meditating?"

In later sessions, Jordan got clear on where she wanted to be one year from now, three years, five years, and ten years. She described her ideal day and thought back to the last time she felt healthy and fulfilled. She described what that looked like and what she was doing. Then, I asked her to imagine herself six months down the road coming back to me to report her success in detail.

Once Jordan knew the direction she wanted to take, she made her vision board. And, you know what? Once she got clear on what she wanted to do, life could come at her fast! She worked on a plan to make the launch, which included building her website; researching similar companies; figuring out costs, fees, and programs; reaching out to potential clients; and, this is a big one, staying accountable to me and her other accountability partners. This clear path didn't leave any room for the fear factor.

Jordan launched her nutrition business in record time! She achieved her short-term goal of having five-plus ladies join her Master Your Macro program, and six of them signed up for her one-on-one nutrition coaching. Jordan's confidence grew with each small success. She attributed her ability to follow through on her plan to being clear on what she wanted and staying accountable. In the process, she stopped talking herself out of everything she wanted to accomplish.

In addition to her new side gig, Jordan managed a full-time job in marketing and was planning her wedding. Sometimes, she'd reach out to me in frustration, which I told her was to be expected. To remotivate herself, she just needed to go back to her "why." She'd bring to mind all her clients' successes and wins, and her face would light up with renewed motivation.

Running a side gig with a full-time job while planning a wedding wasn't easy, but Jordan was motivated, and she made it work because she was pursuing a passion. It wasn't as much about making more money as it was about the abundance of wealth showing up in her life—beyond a paycheck.

Know Your Worth

Many women have difficulty recognizing their worth. Finances, education, and experience all come into play. Even today, in 2020, women are still earning less than men. But learning to fight for what you're worth is about more than just asking for more money. It's about truly understanding and valuing your skills and personal attributes. You bring something to the table that no one else can, and once you truly grasp that about yourself, you will be motivated to insist that you be valued for your worth. The best way to do that is to increase your self-understanding and self-awareness of your strengths and desires.

Here are four questions that can help motivate you to understand and fight for your worth that you can respond to in your journal:

- What do I do? For example, "I am an experienced writer and content creator with 20 years' experience, with a focus on health and wellness content."

- What is unique about what I do? For example, "I have excellent organizational abilities and can see the big picture *and* the minutiae."

- What don't I do? For example, "I am a content creator for social media platforms, but I am not a social media robot who posts daily for a client."

- How do others see me? For example, "Clients see me as a valuable addition to their team."

The examples I gave are brief, but I want you to get as detailed as possible. Once you figure out what you do and don't bring to the table, the next step is to begin to accept those things without judgment—the good, the bad, and the ugly. Give yourself a boost of self-acceptance to keep you motivated to do what you do best.

MONEY TALKS, BUT . . .

I know people with a ton of money who are miserable, and I know people with little money who are very happy and enjoy deep relationships. I bet you do, too. Clearly, money doesn't fulfill *all* our needs. In college I took a basic psychology class, and one theory we learned was Maslow's hierarchy of needs. The hierarchy is generally displayed as a pyramid. At the bottom are life's most basic needs, such as food, water, warmth, and rest. As you move up, you'll start to want shelter, security, and safety. Another step up is love, belonging, and relationships. As you get closer to the top of the pyramid, it gets a tad more complicated; people start searching for esteem needs, such as appreciation and respect. The top of the pyramid is self-fulfillment, or achieving one's full potential.

Draw a pyramid in your journal and divide it into five groups, starting from the bottom.

In your journal, jot down how your needs are being met in each category. If they aren't being met, journal about what you are motivated to do to get them met. Revisit this pyramid often to see how you're doing.

- SELF-FULFILLMENT
- ESTEEM NEEDS
- LOVING AND BELONGING
- SAFETY
- BASIC

BUILD YOUR WORTH

We didn't have a lot of money growing up; my mom raised my brother and me as a single parent. During my middle school years, I desperately wanted a pair of Jordache jeans, but it was hard enough to keep bread and toothpaste in the house. So, fancy designer jeans (back then, mind you) were not part of my future. Even so, some of those most challenging times with my family were my most memorable times. One of my fondest memories was spending one week each summer at Mullett Lake in Michigan with my grandma and grandpa. Those long summer days and warm nights on the lake with my mom, brother, and grandparents were magical. My mother and grandparents made time for my brother and me because they knew that would fuel loving memories to this day.

When you're trying to juggle a career and family, it's easy to feel stressed out and frustrated with the people closest to you. I mean, they're family, after all. But if you're looking for a way to build your personal worth, there's no better place to start than with your family. Not everything has to be about getting in more hours at the office!

Each week, perform each of these tasks with consistency:

1. Have at least one meal a week together (phones turned off). I guarantee you'll be surprised by how gathering around a table to share food can lead to engaging, funny, fulfilling conversations. (If you live in different states, jump on a weekly Zoom.)

2. Go for a walk together after dinner once a week.

3. Read to your kids (if you have them) at least once a week.

4. Smile when you come home and whenever you see the people you live with.

Remember, money won't fulfill your love and relationship needs. Sure, you can buy the people you love nice things, but your time is more valuable.

Understand Your Story

You have a story to share. I've shared parts of my story and several of my clients' stories. When I talk to companies, brands, and business owners, I encourage them to share their stories. A story brings us to life for other people so they can empathize and relate. The idea of being better understood by others is a great motivator for figuring out your own story.

When you know your story inside and out, you'll find it easier to express yourself in your business and personal life. You'll be able to talk to your boss about why you deserve that promotion, speak with your company about making changes in your workplace, or meet with potential investors or clients as you start that side hustle you've been dreaming about. You can even talk to your kids (and grandkids) about your accomplishments in life.

So, how do you figure out your story? You'll need your journal for these next few exercises.

WHO ARE YOU?

One of the biggest hurdles to self motivation is understanding who you are in all aspects of your life. While this existential question is a massive mountain to tackle, all it takes is putting one foot in front of the other.

Start taking the steps by answering the following questions in as much detail as you can. This isn't only about your career and concept of wealth. Consider every aspect of your life as you answer:

1. Who do you think you are?

2. What would you change about yourself if you could?

3. What makes you angry?

4. What motivates you to work hard?

5. What is your proudest accomplishment in your career?

6. Who is your superhero?

7. What do you do for fun?

8. What did you want to be when you grew up?

9. Are you doing it now? If not, what hurdles were in your way? If so, what hurdles did you have to overcome to get there?

10. If you could choose to do anything for a day, what would you do?

WHAT FUELS YOUR GAS TANK?

What gets you out of bed every morning? In chapter 2, we discussed extrinsic and intrinsic motivation. Extrinsic motivation is all about the money, the praise, the fancy house on the hill, and so on, while intrinsic motivation results from wanting to feel fulfilled by the experience.

Are you working to make a difference or to earn an income—or both? There's no right or wrong answer to that question, but it is a question you need to ask yourself about your career so that you know what motivates you to get out of bed in the morning. For example, I love coaching women and seeing them grow. I'm intrinsically motivated. I have the confidence and clarity I need to do my work. Running a successful business and having what I need to live comfortably is my extrinsic motivation, but I hate the accounting side of my business. I'm not motivated to crunch numbers, so I hired out.

In your journal, jot these two words at the top of a fresh page: *confidence* and *clarity*. What's the first thing that comes to mind? Write whatever that is.

Now, consider and answer the following:

• What are you confident about in your career or business?

• What do you have clarity on?

• What aren't you confident about?

• What aren't you clear on?

• What would more confidence do for you in your career or business?

• What would you like more clarity on?

WHAT ARE YOUR VALUES?

In chapter 4, you chose your top-five core values, but now we're going to look at values from a career perspective. Could your personal values be the same as your career values? They may very well be, but I want you to do this exercise anyway. You might be surprised. Your career values represent what's important to you specifically with regard to your work and how meaningful it is to you. Take these steps:

1. Do an internet search for "Examples of Core Values."

2. Review the list and choose anywhere from 15 to 30 values that resonate with you regarding your work life and write them down.

3. Group similar values together into five groups.

4. Review each group and choose one value that resonates with you the most from each group.

5. Write the heading "My Work Values" and list your top-five picks.

Here's one of my clients' top picks as an example: Making a difference, Reliability, Positivity, Honesty, and Tolerance. Now consider your present work life. Are your career values aligned with the job you have? If not, it's time to reevaluate. I am not saying you should quit your job, but knowing what you value in your career can motivate you to make changes. With regard to your job, ask yourself these questions:

• Which values are present?

• Which values are not present?

• Can I make changes so that my career values are aligned with what I am currently doing?

• Do I need to reevaluate my future in my current position?

Asking yourself questions like this may seem scary, but they can motivate you to push yourself out of your comfort zone and live your values in your career.

The Five-Year Plan

I love setting goals, notably a one-year goal, a five-year goal, and a ten-year goal. What's great about setting goals is that when you feel your motivation wane, your goals help you keep your eye on the prize!

Pull out your journal and visualize yourself in your *ideal* career five years from now, then respond to the following:

- Have you switched careers?

- What type of career do you have? What's your position in the company?

- Describe the work you do in detail.

- Who do you work with? Who are your coworkers and boss? Are you the boss babe? Who works for you? What do they do? What are they like?

- Who are your clients? What service are you providing?

- Where do you spend your work time? In an office? On a beach with your laptop? At home?

I know it may look impossible or scary right now, but if you don't put it out in the universe, you may never know what you can do!

WRITE YOUR SKILLS MANIFESTO

Having the skills you need to do a job or even everyday tasks is what makes you confident and independent in life. Every career requires a skill set; some overlap and some are unique.

On a fresh page in your journal, respond to the following:

- List all your business and interpersonal skills.

- How do you use these skills every day?

- What goal do these skills help you accomplish?

Now, use this information to write your skill-set manifesto by stating your goal, what you do, and the skills you provide. Here's my example for inspiration:

"My goal is to empower all women to harness their inner strength and find freedom through change. As a mindset coach, I am a good listener and communicator. I know how to motivate my clients individually, help them set goals, motivate them when they are struggling, and celebrate their successes."

I have rewritten this so many times, so don't freak out if yours is a little shaky right now. Keep working on it. The idea is to have something to repeat to yourself every day. Knowing what you're skilled at can help you move toward your five-year plan with confidence and motivation. It can also motivate you to learn any new skills you might need along the way!

DEVELOP YOUR FRAMEWORK

With all the information you've just gathered about yourself with regard to your career, you can start building your framework for getting where you want to be.

1. Know your end goal. That's your five-year plan—a career that aligns with your values.

2. Know what you bring to the table (your skill-set manifesto).

3. Research and learn any new skills you might need.

4. Set specific benchmarks for yourself to accomplish smaller goals to reach your outcome.

Now, build upon your skill-set manifesto by including more specifics about how you will accomplish your goals. Here's an example of my framework that I've added to my skills manifesto:

By having retreats four times a year in places like Costa Rica, Tulum, Mackinac Island, and Destin, Florida, I will teach women these skill sets through my one-on-one coaching and six-week group coaching program. It is time to create a world run by fearless and unstoppable women who aren't governed by fear or perceived obstacles.

You don't need to show this to anyone. This is just for you, to keep you focused and motivated!

Put Yourself Out There

After I graduated from my master's program, I sent out many résumés, but nothing was really touching my soul. Then, during the 2012 Ironman World Championship, I was sitting on the dock watching the swimmers get ready to start, and that gun went off—for them and in my head. I had an aha moment: It was time to put myself out there in a different way. I had a drive to help triathletes and, eventually, women from all different backgrounds find their inner champion. I knew it would fuel my soul, and I was motivated to make it happen no matter what obstacles might be in my way.

Where can you find similar motivation? You start by taking risks, being okay with failure, and being aware that you don't (and shouldn't have to) know everything. This is where the drive begins! Let's look at each of these motivational strategies now.

TAKE A RISK

Leaping into something new, such as a new career, asking for a promotion or for more responsibility, or starting a business can be risky. When I turned down a full-time position with benefits to start my own business, I knew I was taking many risks. How did I stay motivated? I knew what I wanted. I had my vision board, my five-year plan, and an earlier version of my skill-set manifesto, so I had what I needed to keep me motivated to stay on track—and now you do, too, because you've also been working on those tools.

Here are simple steps to keep yourself motivated when taking a risk in business (and in life):

1. **Accept that everything may not go as planned.** Taking a risk doesn't mean everything will work out the way you want it to. For example, if you apply for a promotion, you may not get it. But now you know and can focus your attention on some other way to grow.

2. **Educate yourself.** Know what the risk requires. Before you ask for that promotion, for example, research what you need to do to make that happen or find out exactly what they are looking for.

3. **Make your own decision.** Your family and friends are amazing, but they are not living your life. They might want to weigh in and caution you to be careful, but, ultimately, taking a risk is *your* decision.

4. **Trust your gut.** If you feel instinctively that something is right or wrong for you, trust yourself and take the appropriate action.

5. **Know when to change course.** If things don't go the way you planned, maybe you want to try again or maybe you need to set a new goal and take a different risk.

To stay motivated, always remind yourself *why* you are taking a risk. Look back at your five-year plan.

YOU FAILED—NICE WORK!

Maybe you didn't get the promotion. Maybe the last time you tried to start a business it didn't really get off the ground. Trust me, I know how this feels. You thought you were motivated and dedicated, but you failed and now your ego is telling you that you will never succeed. Stop! Let's figure out what's going on. What lessons have you learned?

- Did you take the time to educate yourself in that field or area?

- Were you lacking passion for that project or endeavor?

- Did you ignore feedback, letting your ego get in the way? Sure, you ultimately have to make the decisions, but feedback from mentors, coaches, coworkers, bosses, clients, customers, and, yes, even friends and family can be invaluable!

- Were you too distracted? Were you more concerned about your social media presence than your accounting books? Or more concerned about being perfect than being proficient?

It's *never* easy figuring out why things happened the way they did, and failing is never fun. But failure has been one of my favorite lessons. Let it be yours, too. Knowing why you failed will motivate you to try again, because then you know what not to do or what more you need to do.

ADMIT YOU DON'T KNOW EVERYTHING

You are a kid in class, and your teacher asks a question. You sink down in your chair hoping she doesn't call on you. You're scared to admit that you don't know. Maybe that's because you didn't do your homework and you really *should* know. But you're not a child who didn't do her homework. You are an adult, and you aren't expected to know everything. Saying, "I don't know," can be super powerful.

Here's how the three simple words "I don't know" can work for you in your business life:

- A client or boss asks you a question. You respond, "I don't know the answer, but I'll research that for you." Then do the research and come out ahead with additional knowledge.

- You don't know bookkeeping? Graphic design? Or something else you need to get the job done? This is an opportunity to build strong relationships with people who *can* do those things. You can't be everything for everybody.

Admitting that you don't know makes you real in business and in life. Show up every day, regardless. That will take the pressure off and motivate you to learn more and get support from others to make your goals a reality.

Mirror What You Seek

You have a friend or mentor you admire (she's funny, confident, successful, and has great business relationships, etc.), and you wish you could be more like her. You don't need to just wish for it. You *can* be more like her! Instead of saying, "I wish I could be her," identify what it is about her that you admire specifically. Her work ethic, her passion, her know-how, her devotion, all of the above?

In your journal, jot down all the qualities you admire about that friend or mentor. Write down some ways you can bring those or similar qualities into your life to achieve your own goals. Now, literally stand in front of a mirror or use your phone camera in selfie mode. Name your friend or mentor, and repeat a statement such as the following example five times:

"Conny has strong business skills and always seems to make the right decisions. Universe/God, I am asking for the strength you gave Conny so that I can make the best decisions to crush my business. I will consider all the decisions I need to make carefully."

When you go from *wishing* to be a certain way to asking for what you need from your higher power and being *willing* to take the steps, the changes you *wish* to make will become the changes you *will* make. (If you're uncertain about speaking to a higher power, I've got you covered in the next chapter.)

Remember, you won't do everything exactly the way your friend or mentor does it, and you won't end up having a carbon copy of her life. And why would you want to? If you still do, it's time for the next strategy.

ACCEPT YOURSELF

Self-acceptance is an ongoing process. The older I get, the more I accept who I am and I will not apologize for it. I love to dance and take selfies. I love to sing even though I'm not very good at it. I love empowering others. I love to run! What makes me happy is not for everyone, but I'm not living my life for other people; I live my life for myself.

As much as you may aspire to be like someone you admire, you need to start by accepting yourself. Here's how:

1. **Recognize who you want to be.** Do you want to be an employee, or do you value the freedom, as I do, of your own business? What works for you? Who do you want to be in your career?

2. **Know your strengths and weaknesses.** I am good at coaching, marketing, speaking, and writing, but I suck at accounting. Look at your work life. Are you doing things you don't love because you're not good at them? Give those things to someone else or ask for help.

3. **Find a tribe.** Spend time with family, friends, and coworkers who support you and appreciate your authentic self. (We'll discuss this more in chapter 9.)

4. **Get grounded.** When I'm not feeling motivated to be my authentic self, I take time to ground myself by going outside and repeating to myself, "I am me. I am me. I am me. I am me." This may sound simple, but it calms my nerves and reminds me of why I am here on this earth: to be me. That helps me find acceptance. (See chapter 8.)

Ask for Help

I check in with one of my clients regularly about her progress with regard to leaving her career and going back to school, because she asked me for help to keep her motivated. Sure, asking for help is hard for many people. But according to a story published in *Harvard Business Review*, the more people ask for help, the more successful they can become. So, how do you ask for help? First, let go of the idea that you shouldn't ask for help and thinking, "I can do it myself." Seriously.

Grab your journal and respond to the following:

1. Make a list of what you need help with, such as filing, writing a weekly report, social media, accounting, sending out some products, etc.

2. List people or businesses that are good at those tasks.

3. Reach out to the people or businesses on your list.

It is as simple as that. Let others help you.

FOLLOW-UP

Can you imagine how many disagreements would be eliminated in life if we could read one another's minds? But that would be scary, right? Because we can't know for sure that someone knows what's important to us, we need to ask. When someone agrees to help you, be sure to check in. Here are some tips:

1. Don't start with an apology. "I don't want to bother you, but . . ."

2. Send a brief email asking how it's going. No response? Pick up the phone.

3. Listen to their progress and describe the next steps, if any. For example, "It's great that you made such progress. I'll need A, B, and C by Thursday afternoon, because I need to put together the monthly report on Friday."

Fail Fast

When I started my business, I wanted to do everything, and I was motivated to make it work. But I got a good dose of reality. As part of my business, I put together a strength class for endurance athletes. It got good traction because endurance athletes were craving something different. But the return on my investment was negative. After a year and a half, I shut down the class.

I chose to "fail fast" because I understood this specific package wasn't worth the effort, and I knew I could offer something else that could provide a service to my clients *and* bring me revenue.

If you reach a point where you feel you aren't making the progress you'd hoped to, you may need to answer these tough questions:

1. How long have you been in this situation?

2. Are you getting a return on your investment?

3. What is your hourly rate coming out to? If you don't know, divide the hours you work in one week by a week's income minus expenses. Is it worth your time and effort?

4. Is the hourly rate you are making lining up with what you deserve to make?

5. Is it fueling your fire *and* your bank account?

The great thing about failing fast is that you've just cleaned your white-board and you can now do what you want to do next. Go back to the five-year plan on page 119, and do the exercise again. The sky's the limit. You have a clean slate for your career, your job, your life!

CHAPTER EIGHT

Are You There, Higher Power?

Spirituality

You've arrived here because you're looking for motivation strategies to start incorporating more spirituality into your life. It often takes a back seat to everything else in life, doesn't it? Fortunately, spirituality can be as simple as taking time to observe nature. It can also be about starting a regular meditation practice or being more mindful in your daily life. For you, it might mean connecting with a higher power that you can feel present in your life if you sit and listen. In the course of my spiritual journey, I've read many books and watched many videos, but when I sit quietly with myself, I learn the most.

Have you ever felt that something was missing in your life? I was 30 years old. I had a dream job, along with a fantastic family, was training for an Ironman Triathlon, and had a group of incredible friends. As I was dancing through life, I started realizing something was missing. I started waking up and looking at the world differently. I was out on a bike ride one day, and I looked around. I thought to myself, "I am one tiny human being on this planet. The Universe is so much bigger than my bubble. How can I expand my bubble to become a better me?" I started talking to friends about God, a higher power, and looked deeper into Christianity and Buddhism.

Growing up we didn't go to church. I would go to church with some friends occasionally, but not consistently. I knew there was a higher power, but I didn't understand it. Heck, I am still learning. But let me share a few ways this higher power has made itself known to me in my life:

As I was training for my numerous Ironman Triathlons, I would often see butterflies after losing my grandpa, especially during the most challenging parts of my training and racing. Seeing those beautiful creatures gave me strength. When I crossed the finish line at the Duathlon World Championship in the Netherlands on September 9, 2001, my mom and I were hugging, and we saw a butterfly, and we cried. It was Grandparents Day. We knew my grandpa was there.

In 2009 I had a miscarriage, lost my dad, and then had another miscarriage. I was hurting inside, but this is when I realized there is a much mightier higher power than I could ever imagine. I had *no control* over any of those losses. I headed to church about two weeks after the second miscarriage, kicking and screaming. Why would I f&#&ing go to church? Honestly, I was pissed. I thought God wouldn't let bad things happen. After the service, I wrote down two prayer requests: "Please pray for my brother and me for the loss of my dad. Please pray for me and my husband for the loss of our two babies."

Dr. Prieto, the preacher at the Lutheran church in San Antonio, came up to my husband, Chris, and me to say hello, and I gave him my sheet. He asked if he could read it, and I said yes. After he read it, he looked at us with such amazing grace. When he asked how I was doing, I asked, "Do you really want me to tell you?" He said he did, and I replied, "I am mad. I am mad at God." He said, "Good, you can be mad at family." I freaking lost it. He grabbed my husband's hand and mine and said, "Let's pray."

It was 2019, and I was getting ready for Ironman Florida. I was out running two days before the race. I looked over the beach about 1.5 miles into the run course on Surf Drive. I smiled and said, "Thank you, Universe." Race Day. I swam. I biked. I got on the run, and I got to Surf Drive. I said, "Universe, I need one of two things from you: 1) I need to be first or second in my age group and qualify for the Ironman World Championship again. No ifs, ands, or buts. 2) I need to run my best race ever in an Ironman Triathlon; no matter where I finish in my rankings, I will hang up Ironman Triathlons for good."

I pushed hard that day. I had the Universe on my side. I crossed the finish line that day at a time of 10:47:46. I visualized and prepared that I was going to do a 10:47:23! I had the best race in the 15 races I'd done. I was happy. I saw my family, and I was beaming from ear to ear. I asked them what place I was in. They told me that I'd placed seventh in my age group. Right then and there, I knew that my second choice was what I went there to do.

It has been an incredible spiritual journey, and I know that it is just beginning. We all have different views about the spiritual side. No way is the wrong way.

Have the Conversation

Sometimes having a conversation with the Universe is all you need to get clear on your life and enrich your spiritual side. People don't tap into that enough because they think they don't know how. Remember the book by Judy Blume, *Are You There God? It's Me, Margaret.* Sometimes it's as simple as that to get the ball rolling.

Don't know where to begin, here are two starting points:

• Recognize your creator. In *O, The Oprah Magazine,* Marianne Williamson states, "Think on this: There is a supreme power in the Universe that is bigger and more powerful than your small mortal self. This step makes you humble." I love this. Think about what this means to you.

• Simply say, "Are you there, Universe (or whatever term works for you)? It's me, and I'd like to chat." Often, when I run, I start talking: "Dear God, Universe, Guides, Spirits. I need your help." If you need help, ask for it. The Universe *is* listening.

Remember, this is an ongoing journey, so guide yourself toward what you need and not what everyone else needs or what you *think* you need.

GO BACK TO YOUR FIVE-YEAR-OLD SELF

Did you feel more connected to the Universe when you were a child? Many of us did. Find a photo of yourself at age five. Then, weather permitting, go outside. Take off your shoes and socks and find grass to sink your toes into and consider the following:

1. Look at the photo. Visualize yourself on a playground, sitting on a swing, playing in your yard, or at the lake with your family. Choose a time when you were really happy.

2. Speaking aloud, say the one thing you would tell that little girl if you could. For example, "Jen, you're having a great time playing with your brother at the lake. Mom is smiling and laughing.

Everything is right in the world. You are going to have a great life!" What would she say back to you?

3.   Visualize yourself as that little girl, feeling what she's feeling. Does she feel connected to nature? Something bigger than herself?

4.   When you're done, notice how you are feeling.

Keep that photo in your favorites on your phone, and when you need some inspiration or motivation, go back to that happy girl. Remember when I told you how I used to go up north with my family? That's where I go when I'm feeling down. That little girl will always guide the way.

NOTICE YOUR WORLD AROUND YOU

I didn't start noticing butterflies until I needed them. They would show up when I was on the bike struggling at mile 100. They would show up when I was going through a hard time with my miscarriages. They are my signs that I'm connected to something greater than myself and often help me find direction.

You may not recognize signs like this immediately, and that is okay. Identifying them will be your first step. Maybe you have an animal you are drawn to, one found through meditation, quiet time, a bike ride, or a walk. It will appear when you need direction, which is what butterflies do for me. Want to identify yours? Start by considering these three things:

•   Have you had a favorite animal since childhood? For example, did you love turtles, and everybody started buying you turtle-themed gifts?

•   Do you have a recurring dream about a particular animal? Maybe that turtle isn't in your dream, but perhaps you see dolphins or whales or buffalo.

•   Is there an animal you always see when you're in nature? A cardinal, a robin, a moose?

Happy hunting!

Stop and Smell the Roses

Naturalist John Muir went to church when he walked through the forest. I head to my church every time I go outside for a run or sit outside for my meditation time. When I head to the beach, my soul becomes filled with so much love! When I am feeling disconnected from life, I immediately go outside. I place my hands on my heart, take in three deep breaths and say, "Thank you," as I know that nature will pull me back to myself and why I do what I do.

Spiritual leader and peace activist Thich Nhat Hanh said, "Walking meditation is first and foremost a practice to bring body and mind together peacefully."

It's a simple practice: Spend 10 minutes moving slowly, without a soundtrack, and don't try to make it into a workout. Be mindful of every step, feeling your feet on the ground, smelling the air, etc. Finding spirituality in nature is mostly about being aware of the beauty surrounding you!

TIME TO MEDITATE

Throughout the book I've mentioned meditation, but what if you don't know *how* to meditate? Let me offer a few tips to get you started, but here's the thing: It is completely different for everyone. It doesn't have to be hours; it can be just 5 to 10 minutes. Also, it's important to make it consistent. Pick a type of meditation and set aside time to do it daily for at least a week. If you still don't feel motivated to do it, try a different form.

I've tried a number of different ways to find what works for me, and you'll want to do that, too. Here are my suggestions:

- Use an app, such as Headspace or Calm. These have lots of different meditations to choose from. In my case, after a while, I realized I didn't want the noise in my ears. I wanted to just be, but it may end up being different for you.

- Join a meditation class in your area (you can even do this via Zoom). You don't have to commit. Just try it out. You may find a meditation group that jibes with you.

- Check out YouTube videos on meditation and grounding. Many women resonate with Gabby Bernstein's or Michelle Chalfant's meditations.

- Try simply sitting with yourself (see page 138).

Sitting with myself is my preference. No earbuds. Just me. I start with three deep breaths and clear my mind. If I notice a thought, I honor it and continue. If I hear something, I acknowledge it. Sometimes I focus on my happy place, the ocean blue. I think of the sounds, the smells, the sand underneath my feet. I ask God for guidance during my meditation and allow myself to let go of my thoughts. After about 20 to 30 minutes, I grab my journal. (I got this from Gabby Bernstein's book *Super Attractor*.) On a new page in my journal, I write, "Thank you, Guidance of Highest Truth and Compassion, for showing me what I need to know." I start writing. I just let it flow. I don't erase. I keep writing until I feel the need to stop.

"JUMP AROUND" TO GET GROUNDED

Picture yourself right now: You are walking on a white sand beach with your swimsuit on. The wind is flowing through your hair, the smell of sea salt and sunblock on your body. You hear the ocean waves crashing. You feel alive. This is the feeling of being grounded—being present in your body and feeling connected to the earth. This can help you access parts of yourself that you may not be able to recognize amidst the challenges of life.

One of my clients takes her pups for a 30-minute walk every morning. She recognized that this activity gets her grounded, calm, and present for the day ahead. It helped her do her best creative work.

Aside from digging your toes into the sand and walking your dog, let's look at some strategies for grounding yourself:

- Go for a run or a walk. It doesn't have to be super long. A walk to the store or mailbox might do the trick.

- At work? Head outside, take off your shoes, and walk barefoot in the grass.

- Follow your breath. Breathe in for four seconds, hold for four seconds, breathe out for four seconds, and hold for four seconds. Do this until you feel calm. This is called "box breathing."

- Do the 5-4-3-2-1 Mindfulness Exercise you learned on page 17.

Do any grounding technique that works for you to push away any anxiety that comes up when you are getting ready to express yourself creatively.

CLEAR YOUR MIND, DAILY

I began meditating because I realized I was getting anxious about my life and where it was going. I wanted to control everything, but I knew I had to stop and trust the Universe. Developing a daily meditation practice will give you the most benefit. I know it has for me. It's not as difficult as you might think:

1. Pick a time to meditate and stick to it every day. Mornings are ideal for most people.

2. Set a timer for short intervals at first. Even two minutes is a great start.

3. Don't get caught up in correct posture. Sit in a chair, on a couch, cross-legged on the floor. Whatever works for you.

4. You don't need to do anything in particular. Listen to your breath, focus on a spot in front of you, repeat a mantra . . .

Finding Your Higher Power

When I think of a higher power, I think of God, the Universe, my Guide. We all have different ways of looking at and connecting with a higher power. Many people don't believe in a higher power at all. That's what works for them. But if you're reading this with interest and want the motivation to find yours, here are a few things to try:

1. **Embrace an open mind.** Be open to spiritual discoveries. Don't discount small signs and messages.

2. **Meditate.** This can clear your mind enough to hear the whispers of your higher power. Unsure of your next move? Your higher power might have the answer, and you just need to listen.

3. **Pray.** Ask for what you want, and you might just get it, or something that will serve you better. When that happens, you know you're connected.

4. **Help others.** This can help you recognize the goodness in yourself and others. Goodness and kindness can be a higher power, too.

SOOTHING SOUNDS OF MUSIC

I grew up in a musical household. We were always singing and dancing around the house and jamming in the car on our trips. Heck, I was five years old when I went to my first concert, Neil Diamond! Music can resonate deep within us. It can play a significant role in your spiritual life and invite in your higher power. Think about this:

- Is there a song or music that reminds you of someone special and makes you feel warm inside?

- Is there a piece of music that fuels your soul and gives you a deep sense of peace?

- Do certain lyrics resonate with you and have significance in your life?

When you are feeling like you want to connect to your higher power, grab those headphones and play one of those songs.

OPEN THE MIND GATES

An open mind is about being able to understand different ideas or ways of thinking. When I started my spiritual journey, it ranged from learning about Christianity and Buddhism to "just being." I learned some deep lessons because I opened my mind. I learned what worked for me. What might work for you?

Here are just a few ideas:

- Read religious scriptures of the faiths or traditions you are interested in.

- Learn more about guides and angels.

- Check out tarot cards and other oracle decks.

- Talk to friends about their spiritual paths.

- Watch documentaries or movies about spirituality.

The key to opening your mind is to educate yourself about various spiritual paths and find which one or which combination resonates with you. Because let's be real, you can't always read the Bible, go to a fortune-teller, or chat with a friend if you are struggling with motivation and guidance. Opening your mind and exploring all the options will allow you to figure out what motivates you on your spiritual journey.

Get Comfortable Sitting with Yourself

Do you need to keep yourself busy all the time or have a glass of wine even when you are alone? There's no judgment there, but alcohol does dull the mind, and you can't hear your inner thoughts as easily and can't receive the spiritual guidance you are seeking.

I personally would always look for distractions before I started sitting with myself. Even then it was hard to learn how to do. If you still find it uncomfortable to just be and sit with yourself, start small. Here's a strategy:

1. Next time you're ready to head to your next task or about to scroll through social media, stop and take a seat.

2. Set a timer for two minutes and just sit. Don't do anything.

3. If you notice a thought, reflect on it without judgment. Be kind to yourself and give yourself grace.

4. Did you hear anything on the outside? Birds, the wind, kids, the dog barking, your breath?

5. What did you hear on the inside? Was your mind talking? What was it saying? Was it being Positive Polly or Negative Nancy?

6. What did you hear beyond your mind? Did it come to you as a feeling? A random thought you didn't expect? What was it?

7. When the timer goes off, go on to your next task. When you finish that, do this exercise again, this time for three minutes. Increase the time between tasks until you are sitting with yourself for at least five minutes.

Keep Searching

Your spiritual journey is an *ongoing* journey. It is about trying to improve yourself daily and making the right choices. There may be "seasons" in your life when you are flying high and crushing it or seasons when you are struggling to get out of bed. Whatever path you are on, it is the right path for you. Understanding that is part of the spiritual journey.

You may be motivated to do some soul-searching now, and if so, I'm cheering you on. If this is an area of life where you want to feel more motivated and connect with something bigger than yourself, you might be wondering how you will know if you are making some headway. You'll know in your heart, but if you want some data to back it up, ask yourself:

- Do material things matter to me less than they used to?

- Do I spend less time with people who gossip or at least dismiss their gossip as unimportant?

- Do I have no tolerance for mean people and hate-mongers?

- Do I crave meaning in my life and situations?

- Do I seek out opportunities to fulfill my purpose?

- Have I released old friendships and started making new connections?

- Do I recognize signs and symbols and follow their guidance?

- Do I receive insight from my higher power?

- Do I trust the Universe to have my back?

There are no wrong answers here. Just keep up the search. Never stop figuring out who you are and who you strive to be. Your spiritual life will motivate you to harness your inner strength and embrace change.

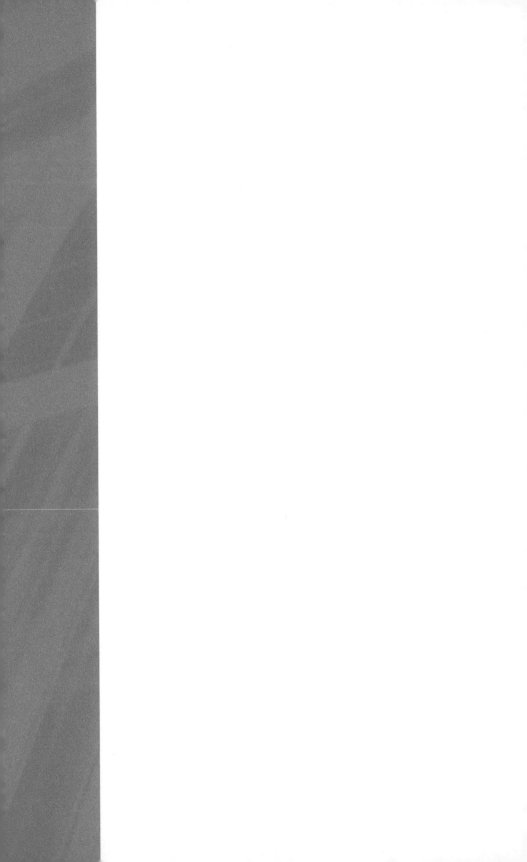

CHAPTER NINE

Community Isn't Just a TV Show

Volunteering, Donating, Taking a Stand

As humans, we learn how crucially important it is to be around other people, whether that's in the office, hanging with friends at the gym, or going for a walk with your partner. Studies show that people who have more social interactions are happier on average than those who have less interactions with others. That's some powerful motivation! In this chapter, we'll look at ways you can become part of a community and grow your opportunities to make connections, make a difference, and be part of something bigger than just you.

MEET BETHANY

The world as we know it is changing right before our eyes, and there are so many people these days who are standing up for their and others' rights—whether it is the Black Lives Matter or the Me Too movement, or something on a smaller scale. According to an article in the *New York Times* on July 3, 2020, Black Lives Matter may be the most massive movement in US history. On June 6, 2020, BLM peaked when half a million people turned out in almost 550 places to protest.

The Black Lives Matter movement played a massive role in my client Bethany's life. Bethany is a nurse with five beautiful kids who went through a divorce after 12 years and decided to start running as a form of therapy. She did her first marathon, 26.2 miles, at 43 years old; she did her first century bike ride (100 miles) at 44 years old; she did her first sprint triathlon and Olympic distance triathlon at 45 years old; and she did her first Ironman 70.3 Triathlon at 46 years old. And that's where I came in.

I started working with Bethany on the triathlon coaching side and got her to a couple more Ironman 70.3 Triathlons and her first full-length Ironman Triathlon at 47 years old. I was out on that race-course with her as her coach in 2018, finding her on different parts of the course. When she had about 1.5 miles left, she was smiling and looked so happy but was falling behind. I told her to get her ass in gear, and she did. She gave me that look of determination and crossed the finish line of her first Ironman Triathlon with a smile. Happy athlete. Happy coach.

Bethany told me that running was the best therapy she'd ever done. It had helped her find her tribe, and she felt she was the best version of herself because of it. Then, on May 7, 2020, as many runners (including me) did, Bethany dedicated her morning run to Ahmaud Arbery for 2.21 miles.

A couple of days later, she joined runners across the country to run for him again. Not long after that, the news of Breonna Taylor broke, and she decided to dedicate her next run to her. It was then and there that she decided to dedicate every run going forward to a victim of racism, lynching, or police brutality. On September 5, 2020, Bethany hit the 300-mile mark. Each run was shared on multiple social media platforms with the name and picture of the Black man, woman, or child who died unjustly. She hoped that those Black lives, faces, and stories would educate and remind everyone what the BLM movement is all about.

Bethany didn't plan to stop at 300 miles, and she says she will continue doing this until her legs give out or Black people can live without fear of going about their daily lives.

Another friend of mine, Vanessa Foerster, is a mental endurance coach. She decided to start a movement called the Diversity Triathlon Movement to help BIPOC (Black, Indigenous, people of color) athletes who have never done a triathlon get started. She found coaches and brands to volunteer their time to help the athletes. It is a beautiful way to give back.

People are standing up. And it isn't for social media: It's to take a stand for what they believe in. While you may not feel compelled to join a movement, you can still help your tribe and community. Every little bit counts.

Make Community a Priority

During the 2020 lockdown, you may have seen some changes in our environment. In April 2020, MSNBC showed us photos of temporary air pollution drops across the world. At that same time, you may have seen human beings become interdependent and genuinely needing each other. The COVID-19 pandemic has had no borders, which has brought us together to figure out how we can win this challenge and support each other.

Pandemic or not, here are five ways you can do something positive and productive for your community:

- Volunteer to help the elderly in your neighborhood. With the pandemic, many older people can't go out and get the basics they need. This is true for non-pandemic times, too. Reach out to the older folks in your town and ask if you can pick something up for them.

- Donate whatever you have extra of (toilet paper, cleaning supplies, clothing, etc.) to whomever may need it.

- Make cash donations where you can to help the people in your community.

- Speak up on behalf of others who can't speak for themselves.

- Join a movement to show your support.

FIND A GOOD FIT

Volunteer work looks great on an application or a résumé, but let's be real: It has a greater purpose. It tugs at our heartstrings and helps society as a whole. What you choose to do needs to resonate with you, though, to keep you motivated to keep going back.

Using lessons I've learned, here's what you can do to make sure a volunteer opportunity is a good fit:

- Consider the skill you have to offer. Do you enjoy being outdoors? How about Habitat for Humanity? Are you good with computers or communication? What about a tutoring hotline?

- Try to find a position that feels like a hobby.

- Interview the organization just as much as they interview you.

- Find out what the time commitment is, and make sure you have that time.

- Is this a one-time deal or a long-term engagement? What do you have time for? Be realistic!

- Make sure the opportunity speaks to your heart.

- Be willing to learn something new. Maybe the local animal shelter needs a blogger, but you've never blogged before. You might want to try your hand at it if you like to write. Maybe you want to learn about animals, so you volunteer for weekends at the zoo.

- Make it a family affair if you have kids. Volunteer for something that gets your crew involved. A toy drive, for instance, can help your kids learn the importance of helping children who have less than them.

BUILD YOUR COMMUNITY

When I think of building a tribe, there are a couple ways to look at it: on the personal side, with friends and family, and on the work side, with colleagues and coworkers. What kind of community do you want to build? It could be something as simple as a gardening group. You know a few ladies who love to garden, so you start a virtual group for gardening tips and meet once a month at someone's garden. Taking that a step further, you can build a community garden together.

Getting started on building a community is a lot like volunteering. Ask yourself these questions:

- What speaks to your heart? In other words, what are you passionate about?

- Do you know other people who are passionate about it, too? Reach out to them and make a plan to meet up.

- How much time will you spend interacting with your community?

- Is it a closed group or will you invite others to join your community if they are interested?

- Is it a hobby you'll all be pursuing together, is it just for fun, or do you want to make this a learning group?

I love cats and am obsessed with kitties! So I started a Facebook group called "Hot Chicks Who Love Cats." I have around 200 women in there, and all we post about is cats! (Come find us!) Is this my only community and do I devote *all* my time to it? No! There's no need to limit yourself to just one; you can spread your time around.

Step Outside Your Comfort Zone

As you think about volunteering or being a part of a community, you may feel a tad uncomfortable with the thought of trying something new. I want you to look beyond just what makes you feel comfortable. Working with a community outside your usual go-to is equally essential because it's a chance to grow and help different types of people. Maybe you'll want to try volunteering at a soup kitchen or arrange for donations at a local school or even be a cuddler for babies.

Here are a few resources you can use to find volunteer opportunities that might be just the challenge you're looking for:

• Check out the website VolunteerMatch.org. It is super simple to use: You just type in your zip code, and it shows you what's available in your area, in-person or virtually. There are other websites like this, too: AllForGood.org and JustServe.org.

• Ask friends, colleagues, or family members if they know of volunteer opportunities. Some of them may be on the board of a nonprofit or maybe they do volunteer work you might be interested in.

Are you ready to dive in? I am going to share more information on how to stay motivated to connect with your community. But first, grab your journal and write down three places that motivate you to volunteer and then offer your services at your earliest opportunity, or at least within the year.

RESEARCH WHAT MOVES YOU

When it comes to volunteering or building a community, the continuous theme is "what floats your boat?" Is it playing with kitties and puppies at an animal shelter? Is it holding babies? Is it helping the elderly? I made the mistake of not digging in deep before I signed up for one of my volunteer gigs, and I lost interest fast. I wasn't motivated to continue.

To keep this from happening to you, grab your journal and do the following:

1. On the top of a new page, write "Joy and Happiness."

2. Go to town for 10 minutes, making a list of all the things that bring you joy and happiness in life. When I did this, I wrote, "travel, marine life, turtles, hearing kids laugh, puppies, kitties, rainbows, butterflies, coffee, running, working out."

3. With this list in hand, head to the internet and search for "Volunteer for *(fill in one thing from your list)*." For example, I looked up "Volunteer for turtles," and I saw places in Costa Rica, Hawaii, Florida, Australia, and Greece. (Wait, I will be back. This looks amazing!)

4. You will see a ton of websites to explore. Do the research and take notes on what a particular volunteer opportunity involves. Does it motivate you to get involved? Good.

5. What about the next item on your list? Explore that, too, and so on, and then take action.

There are so many opportunities out there beyond the "normal" volunteer opportunities. Dream a little dream. Do you want to join me in Costa Rica?

WHAT YOU BRING TO THE TABLE

Your usual way of operating in the world plays an essential role in building that community or volunteering. What do I mean by that? When you can be who you are, it's effortless. If you are energetic, keeping up with kids will be a breeze. Not a fan of kids or a bit out of shape, well, there you have it. Look for something else.

Ask yourself what traits you have that can be put to good use in a volunteer opportunity. Here are some questions to consider:

- Are you energetic? Maybe you want to volunteer at the Special Olympics or coach a kid's sports team.

- Are you reliable? Being reliable is crucial for nonprofits. So, make sure you have that time commitment. If you can only volunteer on weekends, that's okay. If you can only volunteer once, that's okay, too.

- Are you creative? Yes, you are. Head to chapter 6. There are so many ways to use your creativity, and as you know, it's not just about producing art.

Ideally, you want to find ways to contribute to your community that align with who you are. The community will appreciate you for showing up and being you.

CAN YOU DO IT VIRTUALLY?

When I jumped on the websites for volunteering, I saw opportunities to help out virtually, which is pretty fantastic. If you are proficient on the computer and have solid access to Wi-Fi, many organizations will appreciate the volunteer work you can do for them remotely. For example, maybe you can offer free legal advice (if you're an attorney, of course!) or type a term paper for a person with a disability or hold virtual baby showers for people in the military.

Want to build a virtual community or become a virtual volunteer? Here are some ideas to get you motivated:

- Is this your online community? What social media platform or website will you build it on? How will you engage your community?

- What is your profession? Are there people who need your services but can't afford them or won't ask for help? For example, if you are a therapist, you could volunteer your time at a crisis center hotline.

- Go back to the exercise "Research What Moves You" on page 149, and add the word "online" or "virtual" to the end of your search. Or just type in "virtual volunteer." Again, you'll find lots to consider.

Build the Foundation

Having a community is a powerful tool, but there has to be a solid foundation behind an organization. When you start a community, you have to ask yourself, "Am I all in?" For example, I tried to build a triathlon community in San Antonio. My goal was to get coaches and athletes to come together as one. While it was a good idea, it was hard to maintain, as most of the crew had so much going on with their coaching, training, and jobs. So it became a semi-active Facebook group.

Building that foundation is essential, so how do you do it? Let's look at the five Ws of building a community (we'll take this a little out of order!). Knowing your answers to these questions will help keep your drive high:

1. Why are you starting this community? Is it because you want to help others? Connect with others? Find like-minded people?

2. What are you providing to your community? Education? A platform to connect with like-minded people? A workout venue? A hobby? A support group? A reading club?

3. Who are you trying to connect with? Who do you want to join your community? Women? Parents? Runners? Book lovers?

4. When will you connect? Once a month? Once a week? Every two weeks?

5. Where will you connect? In person? Virtually? Zoom? Google Hangouts?

Also consider if there's room to grow. One great example of this is a homeschooling parenting group inviting in newbies who were forced into homeschooling because of the 2020 pandemic. When you leave room for growth, you are building a community that evolves with changing circumstances.

WHAT'S YOUR PURPOSE?

In chapter 4, you started looking at what it means for you to live with purpose. Let's now look at how you can apply living with purpose to your community, locally and nationwide.

Grab your journal and respond to these questions:

- What do you value most in your community? Equality? Empowerment? The rights of individuals? Conservation? Education? Something else?

- What do you want to be known for in your community?

- Can you make a monetary donation or offer your time to uphold this value?

- Does the idea of fighting for this value fuel your soul?

- Can you find the courage to take a stand?

Here are two examples of standing up for one's values: Colin Kaepernick, the NFL player who first knelt in protest of police brutality in 2016. He kneeled to take a stand for what he truly believed and gave up the dream job. Tarana Burke is the activist who started the Me Too movement as a response to sexual abuse and sexual harassment. She encouraged other women with the same experiences to stand up for themselves.

If you want to stand up for something, make it happen. When you know your purpose, it will fuel you. You'll find the courage you need.

FOCUS ON THE COMMUNITY, NOT YOU

As you start considering what you want to stand up for or what you want to do to help your community, stay focused on who you want to support. When I was younger, I was told that volunteering looked good on your résumé or college application. As I got older, I realized it was more about the community that I was helping than it was about me.

I created my Monarch Mindset Squad on Facebook as a *free* option to connect women. I knew my *why*: I did it to connect with like-minded women who need support, whether from other ladies or me. We all need help. I did it for *them*.

Here's a simple question for your journal:

• Why are you taking this stand, volunteering, or starting a community?

Look at the big picture and consider how *others* will benefit from your actions.

Trust the Process

You've probably heard the phrase "trust the process." What you may not know is that it's attributed to Tony Wroten, a former 76ers guard. It's the strategy that former general manager Sam Hinkie implemented before the 2013 to 2014 basketball season. It's become the rally cry of the fans. Unfortunately, the 2015 to 2016 year for the Philadelphia 76ers was a challenging year; they lost many games in a row. But they still trusted the process so much that they filed for a trademark.

This piece of advice can be used for everyday life and building your tribe. You will go through some tough times, and it sucks. Loved ones and fur babies will pass. There will be losses in life. You may lose a job or end a relationship. You may also feel frustrated or discouraged that things are not happening as quickly as you'd like. Trusting the process is knowing that it takes time to heal from heartache just as it takes time to make a difference.

When you have a community to support you, and you in turn support them, change *will* come. For example, in the Black Lives Matter movement, people are protesting, speaking up, and standing up for Black lives. But change doesn't happen overnight. The stance you take today can make a difference for your children or grandchildren. That's powerful and that's trust.

When you know and like the community you are participating in, it's easier to trust that the actions you are taking will benefit others in some way. Let's look at two strategies to do both.

FIRST, ASK QUESTIONS

Maybe you aren't all about starting a movement; you don't have to be. The goal of participating in a movement or connecting with a tribe is to get to know other people and support them in some way.

Here are some basic questions to ask yourself to start learning about the community that you potentially want to join. Respond in your journal.

1. What is the community or the movement all about?

2. Are you educated about the campaign, community, organization, or movement? If not, start learning. Who can you talk to so you can learn more about it?

3. Does it align with your values and purpose?

4. Do you know someone in the community you can talk to about the ins and outs of what they do? Can you tag along?

5. Do you have an idea of how you can help? If not, ask.

DEVELOP RELATIONSHIPS

When you start volunteering, spending time in a community, donating, or standing up for your beliefs, you'll likely notice that you are developing a deeper sense of connection and strength, which enriches your body, mind, and soul. From organizing a simple workout at a park to donating time at an animal shelter, you'll have lots of opportunities to develop relationships along the way.

What can you do to nurture your new relationships? Here are some tips:

Show gratitude. Express to the people in your community that you are thankful for the opportunity to help or be part of something.

Always add value. Reach out to those in charge and ask how you can be of more help. Let them know what skills and qualities you have that may fit in somewhere.

Be respectful. If you want to tag them on social media, ask if that's okay. Respect their privacy and align your actions with what's expected. In other words, treat others how you want to be treated.

Think of relevant topics to discuss and ask questions. Join in conversations and stay positive (don't be a Negative Nancy). Talk about your experiences in the community.

Show your tribe some love. Not only will they appreciate the support you are giving them but they will also appreciate you.

Build a Strong Community

Even if you'd rather join a community than build one, this is something you may want to consider sometime in the future, so keep these ideas in your back pocket. As I've mentioned, there are a couple of ways to build a community—face-to-face or online—and it all depends on where you are comfortable. You've likely already considered this, so what else needs consideration?

I want us to take a closer look at this advice from the 2011 article "Six Ways to Build a Solid Community" on opensource.com:

Make it purpose-driven. Your community needs a sense of purpose for why they are joining your community. Be sure it's clear.

Focus on your purpose and your members. Remember, this isn't all about supporting you. This is about fulfilling a purpose as a team.

Make thoughtful decisions. Every decision you make will affect the group, so make them carefully.

Have the tools and strategies in place. This will take some forethought. What does your community need to do its work?

Involve and empower your members. Ask what their skills are and enlist their help. Involve them in decision-making and encourage them to voice their ideas.

FOSTER TRUST

Amy Porterfield, an online marketing expert, has helped many entrepreneurs (me included), and she has some excellent advice: "When building an online space or community, your people need to learn to know, like, and trust you." Trust builds certainty. In his TEDx Talk, author Simon Sinek talks about Martin Luther King Jr. He says that people followed King because he had a purpose, a dream, a movement. People didn't follow him because he was a cool guy. They started trusting what he said and what he stood for.

When starting a movement or a community, people need to trust you, and their trust will motivate you to keep going. Here are three tips to help them know they can count on you:

Pay attention to the group members. Check in. If it is an online group, maybe you can connect every Monday, Wednesday, Friday. Send out weekly emails or text messages.

Communicate openly. Be honest about what you are doing and what you believe in.

Give back to them. If they are supporting you, you can support them back by offering your time to help with something that's important to them.

Developing trust is crucial, so that people can support your cause feeling certain that they are valued members who are making a difference or contribution. You know how, just share your heart.

FIND HOPE

Why do we start communities? Why do we become part of a movement? Hope. You see the big picture, and the big picture is way bigger than you. Making change doesn't happen overnight, and maybe you won't see it in your life, but what a way to leave a legacy!

Ask yourself these questions to find hope:

- What do you hope will change?

- Who is this change for? Who will it benefit and how?

- How will your voice and knowledge create the change?

- Will you leave a legacy through your efforts? How will that legacy look?

Maybe you don't have these answers now. That's okay. When you've taken the actions we've discussed in this chapter, you'll be motivated to find them.

Reap the Rewards of a Community

Joining or starting a movement or a community is about being part of something that is more significant than any individual. It can help you find a sense of purpose in your life and help others do the same. When looking at the benefits, look for how the community benefits, not just how you benefit.

Spend 10 minutes of quiet time before you respond to the following questions. Meditate, sit in silence, or go out in nature. Then, grab your journal.

1. On top of a fresh page, write down the goal or the mission of the community or movement.

2. Below that, draw a circle.

3. Inside the circle, write all the benefits you want to come out of this endeavor.

4. Outside the circle, write all the things you don't want for this community/movement.

For example, my Monarch Mindset Squad is a *free* Facebook group for women who want to step it up in their lives. Inside the circle I wrote, "Positivity. Inspiration. Guidance. Educate. Motivate. Tools and tips to help them become better versions of themselves. Open platform to be vulnerable." Outside the circle I wrote, "Negativity. Gossip. Selling Products or Services."

Once you see the benefits you are offering, it is easier to recognize the rewards when they come. Anytime I build a community (and I've built many), I do this exercise to keep me motivated for the prize. If something isn't flowing, I go back to that circle to figure out what is and isn't working. Ask yourself, "Am I all in?" Take a stand. Be proud. Don't back down. Colin Kaepernick's stand to take a knee has spread to hundreds of other football players. Your decision to be all in can spread from one to dozens to hundreds to maybe even thousands or more.

INVEST IN THE LONG TERM

Making an impact in your community takes a lot of effort, and you may not see the results or rewards right away. This is not a one-and-done type of experience. Likewise, it takes time to start developing relationships and really feel as if you're accomplishing things in whatever community-minded way you've set out for yourself.

To stay motivated in the short term, keep your eye on the long term. Here are some ways to keep yourself motivated in the meantime:

1. **Make it a priority.** Set aside time to devote to your community. Schedule it into your calendar. Keep your appointments.

2. **Remind yourself of the rewards.** Remember *why* you are doing this. What is your purpose? How are you contributing? What is the legacy you will leave behind?

3. **Do more research and ask questions—even if it takes you outside your comfort zone.** Learn as much as you can about the people you are supporting. For instance, I support the Black Lives Matter movement, but I'm not Black. So I reached out to some Black friends to better understand their challenges. It was uncomfortable for me, but now I have more knowledge about a community I support.

You know what to do. Now get out there and do it. I promise you won't regret it!

CHAPTER TEN

Staying the Course

Making Good Habits Stick

My goal for this book has been to help you find the motivation to improve your life in every way. But more than that, I want you to experience the change you want in your life. I don't want this book to collect any dust. Keep doing the exercises, keep finding out more about yourself, and keep pursuing your passions. When I work with clients, it isn't just about a change in mindset; it's also about a change on the physical and soulful sides. You can read all day long about changing your perspective, but you need to modify every aspect of your life that isn't providing you with a quality experience.

As we close out this book, let's review the work you've done. But let's be real: I can tell you all you want about personal development and growth. If you aren't motivated to make a change, it isn't going to happen. I want you to want to make a change. Start taking the steps toward your better self. I have your back!

Taking Stock, Again

Let me share something about this book and you. You *are* motivated to make a change. You picked up this book for a reason, whatever that may be—trying to land a new job, lose 15 pounds, start a business, or simply be more present. Did you realize that? Your initial motivation is your desire to change and ultimately achieve your dreams and live the life you are craving to live. That's amazing and powerful.

To keep you motivated, I've offered a variety of self-inquiry exercises, action steps, strategies, and tips. What worked for you? Let's take a look.

WHAT INSIGHTS DID YOU GAIN?

When I'm helping my clients in my mindset coaching business, one of my essential rituals is to list all of the positive steps they've completed for the week. This step is crucial because it shows my clients how much they accomplished in seven days.

Take a moment to review your journal responses in chapters 1 and 2. Notice all the thought and effort you put in. That's a win! Do you want to respond to those journal questions again? Great! Each time you ask yourself the hard questions, you gain more clarity on where you want to go. Your motivation level will increase because you have the confidence to move forward.

What are the most significant lessons you learned after doing the work in part one? Grab your journal again, and make a list of all the takeaways that supported you.

Sharing your successes with someone, such as a partner, a friend, or a coach can increase your happiness level. If you feel good about what you accomplished in part one, share it!

REFLECT AND MAKE ADJUSTMENTS

Chapters three through nine focused on specific areas of life. Which of those chapters did you most resonate with? Was it one or more? Why? What are you motivated to change?

Look over your journal entries for that particular chapter. Reread the chapter. Do the exercises again! If the first time around was a little thin on action and thought, dig really deep the second time around.

Even if a particular chapter didn't resonate with you because you feel you've got that aspect of life all worked out, choose one exercise you can incorporate into your life to build on the good you've already got.

HOW DO YOU RATE?

On a scale of 1 to 10, with 10 being the best, rate each aspect of your life in your journal:

- Career

- Community

- Creativity

- Emotional Health

- Personal Relationships

- Physical Fitness and Wellness

- Spirituality

What's your total number? Write it down in your journal with the date.

Is the number less than you'd like it to be? Set a realistic date for some time in the future when you want to see an improvement by. For example: "By *(fill in the date),* I want my total number to be *(fill in the number)."*

Now, look at your lower ratings. Which aspects need improvement? Read that chapter again and do the exercises. Start with the lower ratings first. If you are a 2 or 3 in Community, shoot for a higher number like 5 or 6. You don't have to get to 10 right away! Will you ever be a perfect 10 in all categories? Remember the lessons you learned about perfection. It doesn't hurt to aspire to a 10 in all categories, but don't get too caught up. That can really mess with your motivation!

Want some accountability? Send me a simple email at author@jenrulon.com. In the subject line, post your total number now, your target number, and your target date. It will look like something like this: 47, 65, October 27, 2021. Be sure to introduce yourself in the body of the email and share with me what you plan to do to increase your number. Let me know if you'd like me to share your goal with my social media platform to keep you accountable!

Keep at It

I will be the first to tell you that life hasn't come easy for me. So many times, when I was training for an Ironman, I heard comments like, "You make it look so easy. You are fast. You are strong." And while those comments were coming from the heart, people were only seeing the tip of the iceberg. They didn't know of my struggles or frustrations or challenges. The same was true when I was starting my business.

When people talk about their success, they don't usually share their struggles, but we all do struggle from time to time. And sometimes we all want to throw in the towel. I once cried on the phone to my mom, exhausted, fed up, and feeling like a failure in my business. But I kept moving toward my dreams because I have motivational tools and strategies to get myself back up. (PS, there has been more than one time that I have cried to my mom!)

I don't want you to be discouraged by obstacles or by thinking that other women have it easy and things just flow smoothly for them. You have to walk the walk to your success so that you can talk the talk. Women have been overcoming obstacles for generations. We've seen them rise in both their professional and personal lives—and we will continue to do so. That includes you. Who you become will not only enrich your life but also the lives of generations to come.

As I close out this chapter, let me leave you with something I wrote my ladies during my Monarch Mindset Coaching:

"Every day, the sun will rise. As a woman, you need to figure out if the day will slay you OR you will slay the day."

References

CHAPTER 1

AAUW. "The Simple Truth about the Gender Pay Gap." AAUW. March 2020. www. aauw.org/resources/research/simple-truth.

Adichie, Chimamanda Ngozi. *We Should All Be Feminists*. United Kingdom: Anchor Books, 2015.

Angelou, Maya. *Wouldn't Take Nothing for My Journey Now*. New York: Random House, 2002.

Culliford, Larry. "What Is Spirituality?" *Psychology Today*. March 5, 2011. https://www.psychologytoday.com/us/blog/spiritual-wisdom-secular-times /201103/what-is-spirituality.

Edwards, Joyce C. *Champion Leaders: Pursuing Excellence to Win: Essentials for Effective Leaders*. United Kingdom: WestBow Press, 2017.

Nasty Women Posters: Wise Words from Women Who Changed the World. Maine: Cider Mill Press, 2020.

Roosevelt, Eleanor. *What Are We For? The Words and Ideals of Eleanor Roosevelt*. New York: Harper Perennial, 2019.

CHAPTER 2

Cherry, Kendra. "Why Mindset Matters for Your Success." Verywell Mind. n.d. Accessed September 20, 2020. https://www.verywellmind.com /what-is-a-mindset-2795025.

Janssen, Ian, Steven B. Heymsfield, ZiMian Wang, and Robert Ross. "Skeletal Muscle Mass and Distribution in 468 Men and Women Aged 18–88 Yr." *Journal of Applied*

Physiology 89, no. 1 (2000): 81–88. DOI: https://doi.org/10.1152
/jappl.2000.89.1.81.

Rulon, Jennifer. Macro Counting: August 26, 2020. https://jenrulon.com
/macro-counting.

University of Minnesota. "Why Personal Relationships Are Important." *Taking Charge of Your Health & Wellbeing*. www.takingcharge.csh.umn.edu/why-personal
-relationships-are-important.

Warrell, Margie. "Do You Know Your 'Why?' 4 Questions to Find Your Purpose."
Forbes. October 13, 2013. https://www.forbes.com/sites/margiewarrell
/2013/10/30/know-your-why-4-questions-to-tap-the-power-of-purpose
/#33fa3adc73ad.

CHAPTER 3

Breslow, Emily. "The Importance of Sleep Stage Tracking for Athletic Performance and Recovery." WHOOP. March 7, 2016. https://www.whoop.com/thelocker
/the-importance-of-sleep-stage-tracking-for-athletic-performance-and-recovery.

Campbell, Bill I., and Marie A. Spano. 2017. *NSCA's Guide to Sport and Exercise Nutrition: Study Guide and Exam*. Champaign, IL: Human Kinetics.

Cherry, Kendra. "What Is Motivation?" Verywell Mind. April 27, 2020.
https://www.verywellmind.com/what-is-motivation-2795378.

Cincin, Altug, Ibrahim Sari, Mustafa Oğuz, Sena Sert, Mehmet Bozbay, et al. "Effect of Acute Sleep Deprivation on Heart Rate Recovery in Healthy Young Adults." *American Journal of Respiratory and Critical Care Medicine.*, (2015): 631–636. DOI: doi.
org/10.1007/s11325-014-1066-x.

Dye, Louise, Anne Lluch, and John E. Blundell. "Macronutrients and Mental Performance." *Nutrition* 16, no. 10 (2000). DOI: https://doi.org/10.1016
/s0899-9007(00)00450-0.

Fullagar, Hugh H. K., Sabrina Skorski, Rob Duffield, Daniel Hammes, Aaron J. Coutts, and Tim Meyer. "Sleep and Athletic Performance: The Effects of Sleep Loss on Exercise Performance, and Physiological and Cognitive Responses to Exercise." *Sports Medicine* 45, no. 2 (2015): 161–86. DOI: https://doi.org
/10.1007/s40279-014-0260-0.

Gomes, Mary. "Five Reasons to Take a Break from Screens." *Greater Good*. April 25, 2018. https://greatergood.berkeley.edu/article/item/five_reasons_to_take _a_break_from_screens.

Grundgeiger, Tobias, Ute J. Bayen, and Sebastian S. Horn. "Effects of Sleep Deprivation on Prospective Memory." *Memory* 22, no. 6 (2014): 679–86. DOI: https://doi.org/10.1080/09658211.2013.812220.

Jackson, Chandra L., Susan Redline, and Karen M. Emmons. "Sleep as a Potential Fundamental Contributor to Disparities in Cardiovascular Health." *Annual Review of Public Health* 36, no. 1 (2015): 417–440. DOI: doi.org /10.1146/annurev-publhealth-031914-122838.

Lennon, John, Paul McCartney, George Harrison, and Ringo Starr, writers. "All You Need Is Love." In *The Beatles 1967–1970*. Apple, compact disc.

Lewis, Lindsey. "What It Means to Trust the Universe + Why You Should." Mindbodygreen.com. September 4, 2020. https://www.mindbodygreen.com /0-18264/what-it-means-to-trust-the-universe-why-you-should.html.

Luik, Annemarie I., Lisette A. Zuurbier, Neşe Direk, Albert Hofman, et al. "24-Hour Activity Rhythm and Sleep Disturbances in Depression and Anxiety: A Population-Based Study of Middle-Aged and Older Persons." *Depression and Anxiety* 32, no. 9 (2015): 684–92. DOI: https://doi.org/10.1002/da.22355.

Mayo Clinic. "Caffeine: How Much Is Too Much?" Mayo Foundation for Medical Education and Research. March 6, 2020. https://www.mayoclinic.org /healthy-lifestyle/nutrition-and-healthy-eating/in-depth/caffeine/art-20045678.

National Institute on Alcohol Abuse and Alcoholism. "What Is a Standard Drink?" U.S. Department of Health and Human Services. October 9, 2019. https://www .niaaa.nih.gov/what-standard-drink.

Perry, Geraldine, Susheel Patil, and Letitia Presley-Cantrell. "Raising Awareness of Sleep as a Healthy Behavior." *Preventing Chronic Disease* 10 (2013). DOI: http://dx.doi. org/10.5888/pcd10.130081.

Summerville, Amy. "Is Comparison Really the Thief of Joy?" *Psychology Today*. March 21, 2019. https://www.psychologytoday.com/us/blog/multiple-choice /201903/is-comparison-really-the-thief-joy.

Tartakovsky, Margarita. "The Power in Being Still & How to Practice Stillness." *Psych-Central.com*. July 8, 2018. https://www.psychcentral.com/blog/the-power -in-being-still-how-to-practice-stillness.

Tolle, Eckhart. *The Power of Now: A Guide to Spiritual Enlightenment*. Novato, California: New World Library, 2004.

Watkins, Philip C., Kathrane Woodward, Tamara Stone, and Russell L. Kolts. "Gratitude and Happiness: Development of a Measure of Gratitude, and Relationships with Subjective Well-Being." *Social Behavior and Personality: An International Journal* 31, no. 5 (2003): 431–51. DOI: https://doi.org/10.2224 /sbp.2003.31.5.431.

Wilmore, Jack H., David L. Costill, and W. Larry Kenney. *Physiology of Sport and Exercise*. Champaign, IL: Human Kinetics, 2008.

Xie, Lulu, Hongyi Kang, Qiwu Xu, Michael J. Chen, et al. "Sleep Drives Metabolite Clearance from the Adult Brain." *Science* 342, no. 6156 (2013): 373–77. DOI: https:// doi.org/10.1126/science.1241224.

World Health Organization. "Micronutrients." n.d. World Health Organization. Accessed August 5, 2020. https://www.who.int/health-topics/micronutrients #tab=tab_1.

CHAPTER 4

Caiola, Rose. "8 Ways to Practice Self-Acceptance." HuffPost. October 26, 2017. https://www.huffpost.com/entry/8-ways-to-practice-self-acceptance _b_12640812.

Carleton, R. Nicholas. "Fear of the Unknown: One Fear to Rule Them All?" *Journal of Anxiety Disorders* 41 (2016): 5–21. DOI: https://doi.org/10.1016 /j.janxdis.2016.03.011.

Carter, Christian. "LL Cool J At 50+: 'Dreams Don't Have Deadlines.'" BlackDoctor.org. January 14, 2018. https://blackdoctor.org/ll-cool-j-master -yourself.

Coelho, Paulo. *The Alchemist*. New York: HarperOne, 2018.

Coxe, Gary. *Don't Let Others Rent Space in Your Head: Your Guide to Living Well, Overcoming Obstacles, and Winning at Everything in Life*. Germany: Wiley, 2005.

Davis, Tchiki. "What Is Self-Awareness, and How Do You Get It?" *Psychology Today*. March 11, 2019. https://www.psychologytoday.com/us/blog/click -here-happiness/201903/what-is-self-awareness-and-how-do-you-get-it.

Klontz, Brad. "Living on Purpose." *Psychology Today*. September 23, 2013. https://www.psychologytoday.com/us/blog/mind-over-money/201309 /living-purpose.

Miller, Kelly. "What Is Emotional Health & 11 Activities and Assessments to Enhance It." PositivePsychology.com. January 9, 2020. https://positivepsychology .com/emotional-health-activities.

MindBodyWise.com "3 Exercises for Flowing with Your Fear." November 18, 2018. https://mindbodywise.com/blog/3-exercises-for-flowing-with-fear.

Neff, Kristin. "Why Self-Compassion Trumps Self-Esteem." *Greater Good*. May 27, 2011. https://greatergood.berkeley.edu/article/item/try _selfcompassion.

Olatunbosun, Margaret. "13 Ways Living with Purpose Makes You Happier and More Fulfilled." Lifehack. December 23, 2019. https://www.lifehack.org/814085 /living-with-purpose.

Pogosyan, Marianna. "Be Kind to Yourself." *Psychology Today*. February 2, 2018. https://www.psychologytoday.com/us/blog/between-cultures/201802/be-kind -yourself.

Raypole, Crystal. "Self-Sabotage: 17 Things to Know." Healthline. November 21, 2019. https://www.healthline.com/health/self-sabotage#signs.

Selig, Meg. "6 Ways to Discover and Choose Your Core Values." *Psychology Today*. November 4, 2018. https://www.psychologytoday.com/us/blog/changepower /201811/6-ways-discover-and-choose-your-core-values.

Wilde, Oscar. *Epigrams of Oscar Wilde*. United Kingdom: Wordsworth Editions, 2007.

Winch, Guy. "10 Signs That You Might Have Fear of Failure." *Psychology Today*. June 18, 2013. https://www.psychologytoday.com/us/blog/the-squeaky-wheel /201306/10-signs-you-might-have-fear-failure.

CHAPTER 5

Bariso, Justin. "There Are Actually 3 Types of Empathy. Here's How They Differ—and How You Can Develop Them All." Inc.com. September 19, 2018. https://www.inc.com/justin-bariso/there-are-actually-3-types-of-empathy-heres-how-they-differ-and-how-you-can-develop-them-all.html.

Brown, Brené. *Daring Greatly: How the Courage to Be Vulnerable Transforms the Way We Live, Love, Parent, and Lead.* New York: Avery, 2015.

Caldow, Stephanie. "Emotional Agility: Susan David's 4 Steps to Thriving with Change." PositivePsychology.com. September 1, 2020. https://positivepsychology.com/emotional-agility-susan-david.

Carleton, R. Nicholas. "Into the Unknown: A Review and Synthesis of Contemporary Models Involving Uncertainty." *Journal of Anxiety Disorders* 39 (2016): 30–43. DOI: https://doi.org/10.1016/j.janxdis.2016.02.007.

Carpenter, Derrick. "How to Develop Empathy in Your Relationships." Verywell Mind. n.d. Accessed September 22, 2020. https://www.verywellmind.com/how-to-develop-empathy-in-relationships-1717547.

Discovery in Action. "Above or below the Line—Where Are You?" November 12, 2019. https://discoveryinaction.com.au/above-or-below-the-line-where-are-you.

Goldsmith, Barton. "Tips for Preventing Those Big Arguments." *Psychology Today.* February 18, 2010. https://www.psychologytoday.com/us/blog/emotional-fitness/201002/tips-preventing-those-big-arguments.

Goleman, Daniel. *Emotional Intelligence: Why It Can Matter More Than IQ.* London: Bloomsbury, 2010.

Gregoire, Carolyn. "13 Things Mindful People Do Differently Every Day." HuffPost. December 6, 2017. https://www.huffpost.com/entry/habits-mindful-people_n_5186510.

Joelson, Richard B. "Reacting and Responding." *Psychology Today.* January 16, 2018. https://www.psychologytoday.com/us/blog/moments-matter/201801/reacting-and-responding.

Leialoha. "6 Life Lessons from a Sea Turtle (That We All Can Apply)." Naturally Aloha.com. August 16, 2019. https://naturallyaloha.com/6-life-lessons-from-a-sea-turtle-that-we-all-can-apply.

Moody, Grooters Productions. 2019. "Discover Your Love Language." The 5 Love Languages. March 13, 2019. https://www.5lovelanguages.com.

Runaway Bride. Performed by Julia Roberts and Richard Gere. 1999.

Selva, Joaquín. "How to Set Healthy Boundaries: 10 Examples + PDF Worksheets." PositivePsychology.com. September 1, 2020. https://positivepsychology.com/great -self-care-setting-healthy-boundaries.

Sobel, Andrew. "Eight Ways to Improve Your Empathy." June 19, 2020. https://andrewsobel.com/eight-ways-to-improve-your-empathy.

Spitz, Enid R. "The Three Kinds of Empathy: Emotional, Cognitive, Compassionate." Heartmanity Blog. n.d. Accessed October 1, 2020. https://blog.heartmanity.com /the-three-kinds-of-empathy-emotional-cognitive-compassionate.

Tartakovsky, Margarita. "10 Way to Build and Preserve Better Boundaries." Psych Central. October 8, 2018. https://psychcentral.com/lib/10-way-to-build -and-preserve-better-boundaries.

University of Minnesota. "Why Personal Relationships Are Important." Taking Charge of Your Health & Wellbeing. https://www.takingcharge.csh.umn.edu /why-personal-relationships-are-important.

WomensMedia. "10 Steps to Effective Listening." *Forbes*. July 13, 2018. https: //www.forbes.com/sites/womensmedia/2012/11/09/10-steps-to-effective-listening /#4b7bd8783891.

Zenger, Jack, and Joseph Folkman. "What Great Listeners Actually Do." *Harvard Business Review*. November 27, 2019. https://hbr.org/2016/07/what-great -listeners-actually-do?referral=03758&cm_vc=rr_item_page.top_right.

CHAPTER 6

Berger, Warren. "These 5 Questions Kill Creativity." Fast Company. November 15, 2018. https://www.fastcompany.com/90267859/these-5-questions-kill-creativity.

Brown, Brené. *Daring Greatly: How the Courage to Be Vulnerable Transforms the Way We Live, Love, Parent, and Lead*. New York: Avery, 2015.

Brown, Brené. "The Power of Vulnerability." TED. Accessed October 2, 2020. https://www.ted.com/talks/brene_brown_the_power_of_vulnerability?language=en.

Cohen, Ilene Strauss. "How to Let Go of the Need to Be Perfect." *Psychology Today*. January 12, 2018. https://www.psychologytoday.com/us/blog/your -emotional-meter/201801/how-let-go-the-need-be-perfect.

Cuddy, Amy. "Your Body Language May Shape Who You Are." TED. Accessed October 2, 2020. https://www.ted.com/talks/amy_cuddy_your_body_language _may_shape_who_you_are?language=en.

Deering, Shelby. "8 Grounding Techniques for When You're Feeling Overwhelmed." Talkspace. July 15, 2020. https://www.talkspace.com/blog/grounding-techniques-anxiety.

Devlin, Kieron. "How to Connect to Your Muses: Exercises." Art Heals Wounds. March 8, 2015. https://arthealswounds.wordpress.com/2015/03/08/how-to -connect-to-your-muses-exercises.

Dribbble. "Discover the World's Top Designers & Creatives." Accessed October 2, 2020. https://dribbble.com.

Jeffrey, Scott. "How to Ground Yourself: 9 Techniques to Achieve Instant Calm and Regain Your Center August 28, 2020. https://scottjeffrey.com/how-to-ground -yourself.

Kim, Larry. "9 Ways to Become More Creative in the Next 10 Minutes." Inc .com. August 11, 2014. https://www.inc.com/larry-kim/9-ways-to-become -more-creative-in-the-next-10-minutes.html.

MasterClass. "How to Improve Creativity: The 5 Stages of the Creative Process." MasterClass. January 24, 2020. https://www.masterclass.com/articles/how-to -improve-creativity#the-5-stages-of-the-creative-process.

McLeod, Saul. "Maslow's Hierarchy of Needs." Simply Psychology. March 20, 2020. https://www.simplypsychology.org/maslow.html.

Rowling, J. K. Harry Potter Series. London: Bloomsbury, 2014.

Rubin, Gretchen. "Don't Let the Perfect Be the Enemy of the Good." HuffPost. December 6, 2017. https://www.huffpost.com/entry/dont-let-the-perfect-be-t _b_158673.

Ruiz, Don Miguel. *The Four Agreements: A Practical Guide to Personal Freedom.* Amber-Allen Publishing, 2018.

Sinek, Simon. "How Great Leaders Inspire Action." TED. Accessed October 2, 2020. https://www.ted.com/talks/simon_sinek_how_great_leaders_inspire_action.

Stone, Jim. "The Creativity Hack You Can Do in Your Sleep." *Psychology Today.* January 21, 2015. https://www.psychologytoday.com/us/blog/clear-organized-and -motivated/201501/the-creativity-hack-you-can-do-in-your-sleep.

Wallas, Graham. *The Art of Thought.* Tunbridge Wells, Kent, UK: Solis Press, 2014.

CHAPTER 7

Ackerman, Courtney E. "What Is Self-Worth and How Do We Increase It? (Incl. 4 Worksheets)." PositivePsychology.com, September 1, 2020. https: //positivepsychology.com/self-worth.

Africa, Maurice Kerrigan. "Knowledge Is Power—But It's How You Put It to Work That Really Matters." Maurice Kerrigan.com. December 2, 2019. https: //mauricekerrigan.com/knowledge-is-power-but-its-how-you-put-it-to-work -that-really-matters.

Bernhard, Toni. "How to Ask for Help." *Psychology Today.* June 16, 2011. https: //www.psychologytoday.com/us/blog/turning-straw-gold/201106/how-ask-help.

Boogaard, Kat. "The Most Effective Way to Follow Up When You Need a Response ASAP." The Muse. June 19, 2020. https://www.themuse.com/advice/the-most -effective-way-to-follow-up-when-you-need-a-response-asap.

Evangelou, Christine. "Fuel the Fire: The 5 Sparks of Motivation." Goalcast.com. September 5, 2019. https://www.goalcast.com/2017/06/22/fuel-fire-sparks -motivation.

Geisel, Theodor Seuss. *Happy Birthday To You!* New York: Random House, 1987.

Gendry, Sebastian. "120 Inspirational Quotes About Laughter." Laughter Online University. September 24, 2020. https://www.laughteronlineuniversity.com /quotes-about-laughter.

Grant, Heidi. "How to Get the Help You Need." *Harvard Business Review.* July 8, 2018. https://hbr.org/2018/05/how-to-get-the-help-you-need.

Half, Robert. "6 Ways to Make a Difference at Work." RobertHalf.com. December 16, 2019. https://www.roberthalf.com/blog/salaries-and-skills/6-ways-to -make-a-difference-at-work.

Hurst, Katherine. "8 Things to Consider When Taking Big Risks in Life." TheLawOfAttraction.com. April 3, 2019. https://www.thelawofattraction.com/things -consider-taking-big-life-risks.

Lancaster, Adelaide. "The Power of 'I Don't Know.'" TheMuse.com. June 19, 2020. https://www.themuse.com/advice/the-power-of-i-dont-know.

Miller, G. E. "The U.S. Is the Most Overworked Developed Nation in the World." 20somethingfinance.com, January 13, 2020. https://20somethingfinance.com /american-hours-worked-productivity-vacation.

PayScale. "The State of the Gender Pay Gap for 2020." n.d. Accessed September 15, 2020. https://www.payscale.com/data/gender-pay-gap#section02.

"Population Census Resources." ILOSTAT. Accessed October 5, 2020. https: //ilostat.ilo.org/resources/population-census-resources/.

CHAPTER 8

Alidina, Shamash. "Understanding the Three Aspects of Mindfulness." Dummies .com. Accessed October 1, 2020. https://www.dummies.com/religion/spirituality /understanding-the-three-aspects-of-mindfulness.

Bernstein, Gabrielle. *Super Attractor: Methods for Manifesting a Life beyond Your Wildest Dreams*. Carlsbad, CA: Hay House, 2019.

Blume, Judy. *Are You There God? It's Me, Margaret*. New York: Yearling Books, 1990.

Brussat, Frederic, and Mary Ann. "Spiritual Practices: Listening." n.d. SpiritualityandPractice.com. Accessed October 1, 2020. https://www .spiritualityandpractice.com/practices/alphabet/view/20/listening.

Cameron, Laurie J. "How to Meditate through Exercise." Mindful.com. August 20, 2018. https://www.mindful.org/how-to-meditate-through-exercise.

Cameron, Yogi. "A Beginner's Guide to the 7 Chakras." Mindbodygreen.com. April 28, 2020. https://www.mindbodygreen.com/0-91/The-7-Chakras-for -Beginners.html.

Connors, Christopher D. "How to Create Your Five-Year Master Plan." Medium .com. June 4, 2020. https://medium.com/personal-growth/how-to-create-your -five-year-master-plan-471f57d7b964.

Detox Center of California. "6 Ways to Connect to Your Higher Power." July 14, 2019. https://www.detoxcentercolorado.com/6-ways-to-connect-to-your -higher-power.

Durkin, Erin. "Michelle Obama on 'Leaning in': 'Sometimes That Shit Doesn't Work.'" *The Guardian*. December 3, 2018. https://www.theguardian.com/us -news/2018/dec/03/michelle-obama-lean-in-sheryl-sandberg.

Greenberg, Melanie. "Does Being More Social Make Us Happier?" *Psychology Today*. December 31, 2019. https://www.psychologytoday.com/us/blog/the -mindful-self-express/201912/does-being-more-social-make-us-happier.

Hanh, Thich Nhat. "Thich Nhat Hanh on Walking Meditation." *Lion's Roar*. September 8, 2020. https://www.lionsroar.com/how-to-meditate-thich-nhat-hanh -on-walking-meditation.

Hurst, Katherine. "Is the Universe Listening? 10 Ways to Be Heard." The Law of Attraction.com. April 16, 2019. https://www.thelawofattraction.com/is-the -universe-listening-10-ways-to-be-heard.

Lewis, Lindsey. "What It Means to Trust the Universe + Why You Should."

Rende, Vanessa. "5 Powerful Indicators That You Are Soul Searching." Mindvalley Blog. September 29, 2020. https://blog.mindvalley.com/soul-searching.

Sehra, Nicky. "Your Crash Course in Spirit Animals and How to Tap into Their Guidance." YogiApproved.com. January 10, 2018. https://www.yogiapproved .com/life/spirit-animals-guide.

Shorten, Andrew. "Synchronicity Signs from the Universe You Shouldn't Ignore." TheLawOfAttraction.com. July 16, 2020. https://www.thelawofattraction.com /synchronicity.

Stoddart, Tim. "Finding a Higher Power—5 Practical Ways to Increase Spiritual Awareness." SoberNation.com. March 18, 2015. https://sobernation.com /finding-a-higher-power-a-personal-account-of-god-and-recovery.

Tartakovsky, Margarita. "7 Ways to Become More Comfortable Being with Ourselves." PsychCentral. July 8, 2018. https://psychcentral.com/blog/7-ways -to-become-more-comfortable-being-with-ourselves.

Williamson, Marianne. "10 Ways to Stay Spiritually Connected." n.d. Oprah.com. Accessed October 1, 2020. http://www.oprah.com/spirit/spiritual-development -and-healing-practices-from-marianne-williamson#ixzz6XIVFoBCq.

CHAPTER 9

Buchanan, Larry, Quoctrung Bui, and Jugal K. Patel. "Black Lives Matter May Be the Largest Movement in U.S. History." *New York Times*. July 3, 2020. https://www.nytimes.com/interactive/2020/07/03/us/george-floyd-protests -crowd-size.html.

Evans, Brandon. "What Do You Stand For?—3 Questions to Help You Find Your Purpose." Medium.com. October 11, 2017. https://medium.com/personal-growth /what-do-you-stand-for-6cdcf280312d.

Fernandez, Rebecca (Red Hat). "Six Ways to Build a Solid Community." Opensource.com. February 1, 2020. https://opensource.com/business/11/1 /six-ways-build-solid-community.

Grams, Chris. "Are You Building a Community or a Club?" Opensource.com. September 15, 2010. https://opensource.com/business/10/9/are-you-building-a -community-or-a-club?extIdCarryOver=true.

Greenberg, Melanie. "Does Being More Social Make Us Happier?"

Kyle. "Why 'Trust the Process' Is Life Changing Advice." A Modern Zen. June 28, 2019. https://amodernzen.com/why-trust-the-process-is-life-changing-advice.

Network for Good. "10 Tips on Volunteering Wisely." Network for Good: Volunteer Tips. Accessed October 5, 2020. https://www.networkforgood.org/volunteer /volunteertips.aspx.

Newburger, Emma. "Photos Show Impact of Temporary Air Pollution Drops across the World from Coronavirus Lockdown." CNBC. April 23, 2020. https: //www.cnbc.com/2020/04/23/coronavirus-photos-show-effect-of-air-pollution -drops-from-global-lockdown.html.

Satell, Greg. "What Successful Movements Have in Common." *Harvard Business Review*. November 30, 2016. https://hbr.org/2016/11/what-successful -movements-have-in-common.

Sinek, Simon. "How Great Leaders Inspire Action."

World Youth Alliance. "The Importance of Interdependence during the Pandemic." WYA.net. Accessed October 5, 2020. https://www.wya.net/op-ed/the-importance-of -interdependence-during-the-pandemic.

Resources

Ackerman, Courtney. "How to Live in the Present Moment: 35 Exercises and Tools (+Quotes)." PositivePsychology.com. September 1, 2020. www.positivepsychology.com/present-moment.

American Association of University Women. "The Simple Truth About the Gender Pay Gap." AAUW.org. Accessed October 9, 2020. www.aauw.org/resources/research/simple-truth.

Babauta, Leo. "Meditation for Beginners: 20 Practical Tips for Understanding the Mind." Zen Habits. Accessed October 5, 2020. www.zenhabits.net/meditation-guide.

Becker, Joshua. "How to Stop Comparing Yourself to Others—A Helpful Guide." Becoming Minimalist. October 24, 2019. www.becomingminimalist.com/compare-less.

Bernstein, Gabrielle. *Super Attractor: Methods for Manifesting a Life Beyond Your Wildest Dreams.* Carlsbad, CA: Hay House, 2019.

Brown, Brené. *Daring Greatly: How the Courage to Be Vulnerable Transforms the Way We Live, Love, Parent, and Lead.* New York: Avery, 2015.

Brown, Brené. "Listening to Shame." Filmed March 16, 2012. YouTube video, 20:38. youtu.be/psN1DORYYV0.

Brown, Lachlan. "Soul Searching: 10 Steps to Find Direction When You're Feeling Lost." HackSpirit.com. June 13, 2019. www.hackspirit.com/soul-searching.

Campbell, Bill, and Marie A. Spano (eds). *NSCA's Guide to Sport and Exercise Nutrition.* Champaign, IL: National Strength and Conditioning Association, 2011.

Chapman, Gary. *The 5 Love Languages: The Secret to Love That Lasts.* Chicago, IL: Northfield Publishing, 2015.

Cherry, Kendra. "Why Mindset Matters for Your Success." Verywell Mind. March 2, 2020. www.verywellmind.com/what-is-a-mindset-2795025.

Cohen, Ilene Strauss. "Important Tips on How to Let Go and Free Yourself." *Psychology Today*. August 7, 2017. www.psychologytoday.com/us/blog/your-emotional-meter/201708/important-tips-how-let-go-and-free-yourself.

Culliford, Larry. "What Is Spirituality?" *Psychology Today*. March 5, 2011. www.psychologytoday.com/us/blog/spiritual-wisdom-secular-times/201103/what-is-spirituality.

Davis, Tchiki. "How to Be Happy: 23 Ways to Be Happier." *Psychology Today*. January 1, 2018. www.psychologytoday.com/us/blog/click-here-happiness/201801/how-be-happy-23-ways-be-happier.

Dolson, Laura. "What Is a Whole Foods Diet?" Verywell Fit. March 10, 2020. www.verywellfit.com/what-is-a-whole-foods-diet-2241974.

Doyle, Alison. "How to Assess Your Career Values." The Balance Careers. Updated October 23, 2019. www.thebalancecareers.com/what-are-career-values-with-examples-2059752.

Fernandez, Celia. "30 Quotes for Strong Women When a Little Self Doubt Kicks In." *O, the Oprah Magazine*. July 26, 2019. www.oprahmag.com/life/relationships-love/g26194014/strong-confident-women-quotes/?slide=30.

Grant, Heidi. "How to Get the Help You Need." *Harvard Business Review*. May 1, 2018. www.store.hbr.org/product/how-to-get-the-help-you-need/R1803M.

Greenberg, Melanie. "Does Being More Social Make Us Happier?" *Psychology Today*. December 31, 2019. www.psychologytoday.com/us/blog/the-mindful-self-express/201912/does-being-more-social-make-us-happier.

Headspace. "Headspace: Meditation and Sleep Made Simple." Accessed October 4, 2020. www.headspace.com.

Iosipratama. "21 Examples of Personal Development Goals for a Better You." *Medium*. August 19, 2017. www.medium.com/@iosipratama/21-examples-of-personal-development-goals-for-a-better-you-7dddcbc2f1b1.

Jackson, Chandra L, Susan Redline, and Karen M. Emmons. "Sleep as a Potential Fundamental Contributor to Disparities in Cardiovascular Health." *Annual Review of Public Health* 36 (2015): 417–40. DOI: https://10.1146/annurev-publhealth-031914-122838.

Mayo Clinic. "Water: How Much Should You Drink Every Day?" September 6, 2017. www.mayoclinic.org/healthy-lifestyle/nutrition-and-healthy-eating/in-depth /water/art-20044256.

Me Too Movement. "Me Too." Accessed October 8, 2020. www.metoomvmt.org.

MediaSmarts. "Women and Girls." MediaSmarts: Canada's Centre for Digital and Media Literacy. Accessed October 8, 2020. mediasmarts.ca/digital-media-literacy /media-issues/gender-representation/women-girls.

Prentice, Andrew M. "Macronutrients as Sources of Food Energy." *Public Health Nutrition* 8, no. 7a (2005): 932–39. DOI: https://doi.org/10.1079/phn2005779.

PsychAlive. "A Guide to Finding Yourself." Accessed October 8, 2020. www .psychalive.org/finding-yourself.

Ribeiro, Michelle. "How to Become Mentally Strong: 14 Strategies for Building Resilience." PositivePsychology.com. September 1, 2020. www.positivepsychology .com/mentally-strong.

Rulon, Jennifer. "Monarch Mindset Squad." Facebook Group. Accessed October 8, 2020. www.facebook.com/groups/273080103963574/?ref=bookmarks.

Rulon, Jennifer. "Hot Chicks Who Love Cats." Facebook Group. www.facebook .com/groups/541076439429102.

Sivers, Derek. "How to Start a Movement." Filmed February 2010 in New York, NY. TED video, 2:54. www.ted.com/talks/derek_sivers_how_to_start_a _movement?language=en.

Souders, Beata. "24 Forgiveness Activities, Exercises, Tips and Worksheets." PositivePsychology.com. September 22, 2020. www.positivepsychology.com /forgiveness-exercises-tips-activities-worksheets.

Stetka, Bret. "Important Link between the Brain and Immune System Found." *Scientific American.* July 21, 2015. www.scientificamerican.com/article/important -link-between-the-brain-and-immune-system-found.

Turner, Julia. "Your Brain on Food: A Nutrient-Rich Diet Can Protect Cognitive Health." *Generations: Journal of American Society on Aging* 35, no. 2 (2011): 99–106. www.jstor.org/stable/26555781.

U.S. Department of Health and Human Services. "Physical Activity Guidelines for Americans." HHS.gov. Accessed October 8, 2020. health.gov/our-work/ physical-activity.

Wallas, Graham. *The Art of Thought*. Tunbridge Wells, Kent, UK: Solis Press, 2014.

Williamson, Marianne. "10 Ways to Stay Spiritually Connected." *O, the Oprah Magazine*. n.d. Accessed October 9, 2020. www.oprah.com/spirit/spiritual -development-and-healing-practices-from-marianne-williamson.

World Health Organization. "Micronutrients." Accessed October 8, 2020. www .who.int/health-topics/micronutrients.

Index

A

"Above and Below the Line"
 exercise, 78, 89
Action items, motivation tool, 31–32
Active listening, in relationships,
 89–90, 91
Adams, Ansel, 28
Adichie, Chimamanda Ngozi, 12
Admitting "I don't know," 123
Aerobic training, 47
 anaerobic movement and, 48–49
The Alchemist (Coelho), 101
Alcohol, consumption of, 44–45
American Association of University
 Women, 8
Anaerobic training, 47–48
 combining aerobic and, 48–49
Angelou, Maya, 12
Annual Review of Public Health
 (journal), 50
Anxiety, control what you can
 control, 52–53
App tracking, water, 44
Are You There God? It's Me, Margaret.
 (Blume), 132

B

Beatles, 25
Bernstein, Gabby, 135
Best friend, becoming your
 own, 15–16
Black Lives Matter movement, 28, 144,
 145, 154, 159

Black Panther (movie), 100
Blume, Judy, 132
Boundaries in relationships, 85–87
Box breathing, 136
Brain health, food for focus, 41–42
Breathing techniques, creativity, 108–109
Brown, Brené, 79, 100, 102
Bubble gum creativity, 101
Buddhism, 130, 137
Build-ons, motivation tool, 31
Burke, Tarana, 152
Business idea, components to
 start, 10–11
Butler, Judith, 8

C

Caffeine, 45
Calcium, 43
Carbohydrates, macronutrient, 42
Career and wealth, 27, 111
 admitting "I don't know," 123
 asking for help, 125–126
 failing fast, 126–127
 five-year plan, 119–121
 knowing your worth, 113–115
 learning from failure, 122–123
 mirroring what you seek, 124–125
 motivation for, 117
 risk-taking, 121–122
 understanding your
 story, 116–118
 values of, 118
Carver, George Washington, 10

Casablanca (movie), 100
Chalfant, Michelle, 135
Chapman, Gary, 90
Choices, learning from past, 16–19
Christianity, 130, 137
Clients (of author)
    Bethany, 144–145
    Jen, 130–131
    Jessica, 78–79, 89
    Jordan, 112–113
    Leslie, 58–59
    Melissa, 40
    Stephanie, 96–97
Coelho, Paulo, 101
Coffee, consumption, 45
Cognitive empathy, 81–82
Communication
    active listening and, 89, 91
    love languages, 90–91
    more than words, 90–91
    PAVE acronym, 80
    responding vs. reacting, 79–80
    tone in, 80–81
    as two-way street, 89–91
    using words in, 79–81
Community, 28, 143
    building a strong, 155–157
    building the foundation of, 151–153
    finding hope, 157
    fostering trust in, 156–157
    priority of, 145–148
    reaping the rewards of, 157–159
    stepping outside your comfort
        zone, 148–151
    trusting the process, 153–155
Compassion, giving yourself, 15–16
Compassionate empathy, 83
Conversation
    clarity in, 84

spirituality, 132–133
    writing feelings in journal, 85
Core values, career and wealth, 118
COVID-19 lockdown, 14, 96, 100, 145
Creativity, 26, 95
    adjusting standards for, 107
    breathing techniques, 108–109
    bubble gum, 101
    drawing or not, 97–98
    dreaming a little, 97–99
    finding a muse, 103–105
    lessons for, 102–103
    perfection killing, 105–109
    removing self-judgment, 99
    seeking inspiration, 100–102
    slowing down for, 107–108
    tapping inner child, 98–99
CrossFit, 40, 88
Cuddy, Amy, 100
Culliford, Larry, 27
Cynicism, releasing, 62–63

D

Daring Greatly (Brown), 79, 102
Determination, turtles, 92–93
Devices, 54
Diamond, Neil, 137
Diet. *See also* Nutrition
    goal of eating properly, 40–41
Diversity Triathlon Movement, 145
Dreaming, for creativity, 97–99
Drinks
    coffee, 45
    health and wellness, 43–45
    soda, juice and alcohol
        consumption, 44–45
    water intake, 43–44
Duathlon World Championships, the
    Netherlands, 130

E

Ego, 88
The Elephant House, 101, 102
Emotional empathy, 82–83
Emotional health, 25, 57
    building resilience, 58–59
    forgiveness, 63–65
    learning to let go, 59–61
    living with purpose, 71–74
    releasing cynicism, 62–63
    self-acceptance for, 69–71
    self-awareness and, 67–69
    self-sabotage and, 65–67
    thoughts, emotions and actions, 69
Empathy, 81
    cognitive, 81–82
    compassionate, 83
    emotional, 82–83
Energy Wreaths, 96
Enjoli-woman archetype, 8
Exercises
    building capacity for, 47
    building speed, 47–48
    combination of aerobic and anaerobic
        movement, 48–49
    examining your motivation, 23
    health and wellness, 46–49
    learning from past choices, 16–19
    Mindfulness Exercise
        (54-3-2-1), 17, 136
    reviewing successes, 14–15
    setting your goals, 28–30
    what's going on?, 4–6
    your priority pie, 9
Extrinsic motivation, 22, 23. 97, 117

F

Facebook, *vi*, 10
    community, 34, 153
    groups, 63, 148, 151

    Monarch Mindset Squad, 153, 158
Failures
    failing fast, 126–127
    learning from, 122–123
Family, personal relationships, 25–26
Fats, macronutrient, 42
Fear, 66–67
Feelings, writing a letter about, 59–60
Fitbit, 51
The Five Love Languages (Chapman), 90
Five-year plan, 119–121
    framework of, 120–121
    skills manifesto, 119–120
Foerster, Vanessa, 145
Forgiveness
    emotional health and, 63–65
    for others, 64–65
    for yourself, 65
The Four Agreements (Ruiz), 102
Friendships
    audit of, 63
    giving yourself, 15–16

G

Girls Who Code, 7
Goals
    art of being still, 53–54
    creating vision board of, 30
    exercise in setting, 28–30
    writing them down, 29
Goodall, Jane, 12
Grace, giving yourself, 15–16
Grounding yourself, 135–136
Grudge, letting go of, 59

H

Harris, Kamala, 8
Harry Potter series, 101
Harvard Business Review
    (journal), 125

Health and wellness, 39
  art of being still, 53–54
  being yourself, 51–53
  emotional, 25
  exercise for, 46–49
  hydration, 43–45
  nutrition, 40–43
  physical, 24
  self-comparison and, 52
  sleep and, 49–51
  water intake, 43–44
Heart rate, exercise and, 46–49
HHS.gov, 46
Higher power, finding your, 136–138
Hinkie, Sam, 153
Hope, community finding, 157
Hydration, health and wellness, 43–44

I

"I am" statements, 61
IGTV, 10
IIFYM (If It Fits Your Macros), 42
Inner child, tapping for creativity, 98–99
Inspiration
  for creativity, 100–102
  finding a muse for, 103–105
  places providing, 104
Inspiring quotes, 12
Instagram, *vi*
Instagram Live, 10
Intrinsic motivation, 22, 23, 97, 117
Ironman Triathlon
  Bethany (client), 144
  Jen (author), *vi*, 52, 92, 130–131
  training for, 164
Ironman World Championship, *vi*, 97,
    121, 131

J

JenRulon.com/macro-counting, 42

Journal
  determining priorities, 9
  examining motivation, 23
  examining your thoughts, 69
  finding yourself, 87–88
  forgiveness for others, 64–65
  forgiveness response, 64
  forgiving yourself, 65
  hierarchy of needs, 114
  ideal five-year plan, 119
  identifying values, 72–73
  knowing your worth, 113
  learning about community, 154
  purpose questions, 71–72
  rating aspects of your life, 163
  rewards of community, 157–158
  self-empowering
    questions, 99
  tapping inner child, 98–99
  volunteer opportunities, 149
  writing feelings in, 85
Journal of the American Society on Aging
  (journal), 41
Journey, ongoing spiritual, 139–140
Juices, consumption of, 44–45
"Just Do It," Nike, 105

K

Kaepernick, Colin, 152, 158
Kahlo, Frida, 95. *See also*
    Creativity
King, Billie Jean, 12, 156
King, Martin Luther, Jr., 156
Koichi, Irisawa, 48

L

Lao Tzu, 69
Lessons
  live, 102–103
  online, 102

Letting go
  emotional health and, 59–61
  writing "I am" statements, 61
  writing letter to past
    self, 60–61
Library, inspiration, 101–102
Life
  acknowledging good in, 62–63
  audit friendships, 63
  career and wealth, 27
  creative endeavors, 26
  emotional health, 25
  health and wellness, 24, 39
  interrelation of, 23–24
  living with purpose, 71–74
  physical relationships, 25–26
  spiritual guidance, 27–28
  supporting community, 28
Live lessons, 102–103
Love languages, in
    communication, 90–91
lululemon athletica, 10 78

M

Macronutrients, 42
Magnesium, 43
Marsh, Brandon, 52
MarysBreathJourneys.com, 108
Maslow's hierarchy of needs, 114
Master Your Macro program, 112
Mayo Clinic, 44, 45
Meditation, 129, 133, 134
  clearing your mind, 136
  finding higher power, 137
  grounding yourself, 135–136
  time for, 134–135
Me Too movement, 8, 152
Micronutrients, 42–43
Mindfulness
  exercise, 17, 67, 136

motivation tool, 32
Monarch Mindset Coaching, 78, 164
Monarch Mindset program, *vii*
Monarch Mindset Squad, 34, 153, 158
Motivation, *vii*
  career, 117
  examining your, 23
  exercise routines for, 46
  extrinsic, 22, 23, 97, 117
  fear as obstacle, 66–67
  food for focus, 41–42
  inspiring quotes, 12
  intrinsic, 22, 23, 97, 117
  knowing yourself, 116–117
  making habits stick, 161
  for risk-taking, 121–122
  secret to, 4
  self-help book, 6–7
  taking stock of changes, 162–164
  turtles as, 92–93
Motivational tool kit, 30–33
  action items, 31–32
  build-ons, 31
  mindfulness, 32
  one-offs, 31
  reframing, 32–33
Muir, John, 134
Muse, for creativity, 103–105
Music, 137

N

National Institute on Alcohol Abuse and
    Alcoholism, 44
New York Times (newspaper), 144
Nike, 105
*NSCA's Guide to Sport and Exercise
    Nutrition*, 42, 43, 45
Nutrition
  food for focus, 41–42
  goal of eating properly, 40–41

macronutrients, 42
micronutrients, 42–43

O

One-offs, motivation tool, 31
Online community, connecting with, 14
Online lessons, 102
Open mind, 137–138
The Oprah Magazine (magazine), 132

P

Passion, 73–74
PAVE acronym, communication, 80
Perfection
    creativity and, 105–109
    for losers, 106
"Perfect" women, 8
Personal development and
    growth, 161
Personal relationships, 25–26, 77
    cognitive empathy in, 81–82
    compassionate empathy in, 83
    emotional empathy in, 82–83
    empathy in, 81–83
    making the first move in, 84–85
    setting firm boundaries, 85–87
    staying present in, 92–93
    time for building, 87–89
    two-way communication
        in, 89–91
    using words in, 79–81
Physical health, 24
Picasso, Pablo, 100
Pinterest, 7, 30, 68, 93, 104
Porterfield, Amy, 156
Prayer, finding higher power, 137
Presence, in relationships, 92–93
Pressure, feeling overwhelmed, 33–34
Priorities, exercise for determining, 9
Productivity, schedule time for, 13

Proteins, macronutrient, 42
Psychology Today (magazine), 27
Purpose
    finding your, 152
    identifying values, 72–73
    living with, 71–74
    passion and, 73–74

R

Reality, healthy dose of, 10–11
Reframing, motivation tool, 32–33
Relationships. *See also* Personal
    relationships
    personal, 25–26
    volunteering and, 154–155
Resources, using, 13
Responsibility, 9, 13, 79, 121
Rewards of community, 157–159
Risk taking
    lessons from failing, 122–123
    motivation, 121–122
Roberts, Julia, 87
Rohn, Jim, 62
Roosevelt, Eleanor, 12
Rowling, J. K., 101
Ruiz, Don Miguel, 102
Runaway Bride (movie), 87

S

Saturday Night Live (television show),
    character Stuart Smalley, 61
Self-acceptance, 124–125
    emotional health, 69–71
    kindness and, 70
    non-negotiables and, 70–71
Self-affirmation, "I am" statements, 61
Self-awareness
    for emotional health, 67–69
    exercising, 68–69

getting comfortable with
self, 138–139
thoughts, emotions and actions, 69
Self-help book, 6–7
Self motivation, career and
wealth, 116–117
Self-sabotage
fear and, 66–67
insecurities and, 65–66
putting yourself down, 66
Self-talk, 61
The Shawshank Redemption (movie), 100
Sinek, Simon, 100, 156
Skills, five-year plan for, 119–120
Sleep
devices and, 54
health and wellness, 49–51
mental benefits of, 50
physical benefits of, 50
tracking, 51
Sleep and Breathing (journal), 49
Sleep Genius, 51
Slow down, creativity, 107–108
Social media, *vii*, 7, 13, 58
business promotion on, 26
comparing self to others, 52
friendships and, 63
inspiration on, 101
knowing your worth, 113
limiting time on, 62
relationships and, 155
sharing news on, 145, 164
staying present, 92
virtual community of, 150
Soda, consumption of, 44–45
Spirituality, 27–28, 129
conversation about, 132–133
finding your higher power, 136–138
getting comfortable with
yourself, 138–139
ongoing journey to, 139–140

open mind for, 137–138
searching for, 139–140
stop and smell the roses, 134–136
Standard adjustment, creativity, 107
Stay-at-home moms, 8
Stillness, 53–54
Stockton, Mary, 108
Story, understanding your, 116–118
Stress, feeling overwhelmed, 33–34
Successes
reviewing your, 14–15
sleep and, 49
Super Attractor (Bernstein), 135

T

Tabata Interval, 47–48
TED Talk, 100
TEDx Talk, 12, 156
Teresa, Mother, 99
Thich Nhat Hanh, 134
Time (for building relationships), 87–89
checking your ego, 88
finding yourself first, 87–88
freeing your mind, 89
Tone, communication, 80–81
Training, controlling what you
can, 52–53
Triathlons, 7
coach, *vi*, 52
community, 151
Diversity Triathlon Movement, 145
Ironman, *vi*, 52, 92, 130–131, 144
racing kit, 106
Tri Sirena Apparel, 26
Trusting the process, 153–155
Turtles, determination of, 92–93

V

Values
career, 118
identifying your, 72–73

Vitamin B6, 43
Vitamin C, 43
Vitamin E, 43
VolunteerMatch.org, 148
Volunteer work
    community, 146–147
    contributions, 149–150
    online community, 150–151
    websites for, 150

W

Water intake, health
    and, 43–44
Wealth. *See* Career and
    wealth
WeCOACH, 7
Wellness, physical health
    and, 24

WHOOP, sleep-monitoring, 51
Williams, Serena, 8
Williamson, Marianne, 132
World Health Organization, 43
Worth
    building your, 115
    hierarchy of needs, 114
    knowing your, 113–115
Wroten, Tony, 153

Y

Yousafzai, Malala, 8
YouTube, 10, 33, 46, 50, 102, 135

Z

Zinc, 43
Zoom, 10, 96, 115, 134, 151

Acknowledgments

I could sit here and list many people, but I will keep these thanks super simple. Thank you to my SoulFit, San Antonio, family for keeping me sane during this time. Jason's workouts in person and on Zoom are what I needed to move my body.

Thank you, Colorado, for allowing me to feel, meditate, and breathe during our work-cation (with hubby). Your mountains are just what I needed for peace of mind. Thank you, Destin, Florida, for allowing me to ground myself, go through Hurricane Sally, rinse away my fears of being vulnerable, and enabling me to finish my book. Your beaches feed my soul.

Thank you to all my athletes and clients who believed in my coaching. I am forever grateful to you. Thank you to my editor, Carolyn, who was patient with me and made the process so much easier.

Thank you to my amazing girlfriends (you know who you are) who have helped me not only during this book but throughout my life. If it weren't for you ladies, my dreams wouldn't be where they are today.

A huge thank-you to my family: my husband, Chris; my mom; my brother, Chris; my sister-in-law, Vikki; and my nephew, Jaxson, for your forever support. And to the little one, Taryn, my niece. Thank you for showing me the world through your eyes and reminding me that we all need to live life like a champion.

About the Author

 **Jen Rulon** has been a triathlon coach for nearly 20 years and is owner of JenRulon.com. She holds a master's in kinesiology with an emphasis in exercise science. Jen has coached more than 50 athletes to cross the finish line "with a smile." She is also a 15x Ironman Triathlete who qualified and participated in the 2017 World Championship in Kona, Hawaii.

After stepping away from triathlons in 2019, Jen launched Monarch Mindset to empower all women to harness their inner strength and find freedom through change. You can find her expert knowledge in *Men's Journal* magazine, Men's Journal online, the *New York Times*, *Runner's World* magazine, *Triathlete* magazine, and WebMD. You can also stream online her talks from TEDx Talk Stage, the Health and Wellness Expo Stage in San Antonio, Texas, and workshops with TrainingPeaks' Endurance Coaching Summit.

Jen currently resides in San Antonio, Texas, with her husband, Chris, and kitty, OC, where she continues to stay fit through strength training, running, and yoga, but has also learned the art of rest and relaxation, when needed.